A Royal Banquet

Copyright ©2000 Spring Harvest

The authors assert the moral right to be identified as the authors of this work.

Published by
Spring Harvest
14 Horsted Square
Uckfield
East Sussex TN22 1QL

First edition 2000

All rights reserved

Acknowledgements
Scripture quotations taken from the HOLY BIBLE, NEW INTERNATIONAL VERSION.
Copyright ©1973, 1978, 1984 by International Bible Society.
Used by permission of Hodder and Stoughton Limited.
All rights reserved.

Photograph on Page 113 copyright © Howard Barlow

"NIV" is a registered trade mark of International Bible Society. UK trademark number 1448790

Spring Harvest. A Registered Charity.

ISBN 1 899 78831 X

A Royal Banquet

Spring Harvest 2000 Study Guide

by Jeff Lucas

with contributions from Pete Gilbert, David Hilborn, Stuart Murray, and Chris Thackery

Please note that the inclusion of a quotation or example in this book does not imply endorsement by Spring Harvest.

Using this Study Guide

At the beginning of each section is a BIBLE PASSAGE from John's gospel with some notes. These introduce us to the theme of the section. Then there's an introduction and MENU – an overview of the material that follows.

Following is the MAIN COURSE – the body of the material itself. The MAIN COURSE is served up in two-page helpings, and is a resource centre.

The left-hand page contains the main body of the teaching material, with relevant quotations in the left margin. Throughout the text the **?** icon draws your attention to key questions raised by the teaching material. LINKS on the right-hand page contain information that amplifies or illustrates the teaching material.

RESOURCE LINKS
references to books, web sites or organizations

A BOOK.LINK [book.link] is a pointer to a book you might like to read to study a particular issue to a greater depth.

A WEB.LINK [WWW http//web.link] provides details of a web site or page on the internet where you can find further information.

FURTHER INFORMATION LINKS
more detailed material to complement the core teaching material

A PAST.LINK [past.link] is a historical link giving a perspective from history that illustrates the subject.

A PLUS.LINK [plus.link] is more detail, perhaps a newspaper article or research paper that amplifies or comments on the material.

A THEO.LINK [THEO LINK] contains more detailed theological or doctrinal material.

Welcome to the banquet

The theme for this Spring Harvest Study Guide is *A Royal Banquet*. Drawing particularly from the gospel of John, we are going to take a fresh look at Jesus. We chose the banquet theme because we want to look closely at Jesus and his relationships, and so the image of a feast – a lively, energetic celebration of friendship – is appropriate for us.

Our aim is not just to gather information or engage in study. We want to ask some fundamental questions about what it means to be a Christian, about the nature and content of the Christian message, and about how to practice Jesus-centred spirituality in our frantic, superficial world. How did Jesus relate to his father, his friends and his world – and what are the practical implications of his example for us?

Contents

SECTION I

JESUS AT THE CENTRE

"Christians ought to be celebrating constantly. We ought to be preoccupied with parties, banquets, feasts and merriment. We ought to give ourselves over to veritable orgies of joy because of our belief in resurrection. We ought to attract people to our faith quite literally by the fun there is in being a Christian. Unfortunately, however, we too readily become sombre, serious, and pompous. We fly in the face of our own tradition because we are afraid of wasting time or getting attached. In the words of Teresa of Avila: '... from silly devotions and sour faced saints, spare us, O Lord.'"
– *Robert Hotchkins*

"Jesus' good news, then, was that the kingdom of God had come, and that he, Jesus, was its herald and expounder to men. More than that, in some special, mysterious way, he was the kingdom."
– *Malcolm Muggeridge*

"Laugh with me! Death is dead! Fear is no more! There is only life! There is only laughter! ... Laughter is not hysteria. Laughter is not a belly explosion over a vulgar joke. Laughter is ... joy in living ... in the midst of death you are constantly discovering life: in a glance or a touch or a song ... in a field of corn or a friend who cares, in the moon or an amoeba, in a lifeless loaf suddenly become the body of Christ."
– *Eugene O'Neill,* Lazarus Laughed

JESUS AT THE CENTRE

BIBLE PASSAGE

John 1:1–14

In the beginning was the Word, and the Word was with God, and
the Word was God. 2He was with God in the beginning.

3Through him all things were made; without him nothing was
made that has been made. 4In him was life, and that life was the
light of men. 5The light shines in the darkness, but the darkness
has not understood it.

6There came a man who was sent from God; his name was John.
7He came as a witness to testify concerning that light, so that
through him all men might believe. 8He himself was not the
light; he came only as a witness to the light. 9The true light that
gives light to every man was coming into the world.

10He was in the world, and though the world was made through
him, the world did not recognize him. 11He came to that which
was his own, but his own did not receive him. 12Yet to all who
received him, to those who believed in his name, he gave the
right to become children of God – 13children born not of natural
descent, nor of human decision or a husband's will, but born of
God.

14The Word became flesh and made his dwelling among us. We
have seen his glory, the glory of the One and Only, who came
from the Father, full of grace and truth.

Comment

The magnificent, unique Christ

v1 The word

v4 The life

v4-5 The light

v2 Jesus stands astride history as the eternal, preexistent One

v14 The incarnational leap from the throne to the cross/grave. He has pitched his tent among us

Christ is ***the*** message of God

v12 Receiving and believing

v14 Grace and truth in Christ

NOTES

SECTION 1

JESUS AT THE CENTRE

In **him** was **life**, and that **life** was the light of men. John 1:4

whoever believes in **him** shall not perish but have eternal **life**. John 3:16

whoever rejects the **Son** will not see **life**, John 3:36

the **Son** gives **life** to whom he is pleased to give it. John 5:21b

I am the bread of **life**. John 6:35

I have come that they may have **life**, and have it to the full. John 10:10

I am the resurrection and the **life**. John 11:25

Now this is eternal **life**: that they may know you, **the only true God**, and **Jesus Christ**, whom you have sent. John 17:3

But these are written that you may believe that **Jesus** is the **Christ**, the Son of God, and that by believing you may have **life** in his name. John 20:31

JESUS AT THE CENTRE – MENU

The Christian life can become very cluttered. This section takes a look at some of the ways in which the Church – and we as individuals – may have 'lost the plot.'

Having considered how we have excluded the person and life of Jesus from our thinking, we ask the question: "What does it mean to put Jesus right at the heart of our lives – both individual and corporate?"

THE BANQUET

SECTION 1

JESUS AT THE CENTRE

JOHN 2:1–11

1On the third day a wedding took
place at Cana in Galilee. Jesus'
mother was there, 2and Jesus and
his disciples had also been invited
to the wedding. 3When the wine
was gone, Jesus' mother said to
him, "They have no more wine."
4"Dear woman, why do you
involve me?" Jesus replied, "My
time has not yet come."
5His mother said to the servants,
"Do whatever he tells you."
6Nearby stood six stone water jars,
the kind used by the Jews for
ceremonial washing, each holding
from twenty to thirty gallons.
7Jesus said to the servants, "Fill the
jars with water"; so they filled
them to the brim.
8Then he told them, "Now draw
some out and take it to the master
of the banquet."
They did so, 9and the master of the
banquet tasted the water that had
been turned into wine. He did not
realize where it had come from,
though the servants who had
drawn the water knew. Then he
called the bridegroom aside 10and
said, "Everyone brings out the
choice wine first and then the
cheaper wine after the guests have
had too much to drink; but you
have saved the best till now."
11This, the first of his miraculous
signs, Jesus performed at Cana in
Galilee. He thus revealed his glory,
and his disciples put their faith in
him.

THE BANQUET

Jesus out in the cold

John's gospel portrays the Jesus who launched his ministry not in the temple courts or during a debate with important religious dignitaries, but at a party – a wedding in Cana, to be precise.

His opening scene from the ministry of Jesus is a domestic miracle, which was also a sign and a wonder. But the grinning celebrants would have been unanimous, had they known who it was that had provided such wonderful wine – Jesus really was the life and soul of that particular party.

Banquets and parties figure highly in the ministry of Jesus in all four of the Gospels – so much so that Tony Campolo has remarked that Jesus is the 'party deity'.

As Christians, we are not just forgiven and on our way to heaven. We have stepped out of darkness into God's light, and are invited to enjoy a radical new order of existence – a life that begins now and will flow on, past death, into eternity. God invites us to a life that is a Jesus-centred banquet. This doesn't suggest that lives will be untouched by trouble or pain – sometimes God sets a table before us 'in the presence of our enemies' (Psalm 23:5). In this world we will have trouble (John 16:33). But even in the darkest times, we are able to look forward to the eternity where we will celebrate and party in the future that God is preparing for us (John 14).

Uninvited by popular culture

Millennial banquet – happy birthday to whom?

It was one of the largest, most expensive birthday parties in the history of planet earth – the dome alone cost 700 million pounds – and millions of revellers forgot to invite the one whose birth was allegedly being celebrated. A recent poll in Britain asked 7- to 16-year-olds what the millennium meant. Twenty-three per cent said: "It celebrates 2000 years since the birth of Jesus." And 27 per cent said: "It is a reason for adults to drink champagne and have a party."

Dr John Drane, senior lecturer in practical theology at University of Aberdeen, laments:
"As long ago as 1992, I attended a meeting to discuss the most effective ways for the mass media to mark the arrival of the new

BANQUETS

Jesus taught that his kingdom is like a banquet (Matt 22:2). He threw miraculous open air picnics to teach his disciples a point. He attended a banquet held in his honour at Levi's house (Luke 5:29). And Zacchaeus became an exuberant philanthropist as a result of Jesus' inviting himself for lunch (Luke 19:5). Jesus even taught his disciples banquet protocol (Luke 14:7–14).

But in John's gospel, the concept of feeding and banquet is taken further. In John's figurative language, Jesus himself is part of the feast, the very bread of life (John 6:51). Cana is the first hint that Jesus brings the new wine of the kingdom, the abundance of the Holy Spirit.

LIFE IN JOHN

The life of God has been manifested in Jesus Christ – and John celebrates and points to that life throughout his writing. Life as a noun occurs thirty-six times in John's gospel, and eleven of these instances are in conjunction with the adjective eternal. Christ is the 'true God and eternal life' (1 John 5:20), 'the resurrection and the life' (John 11:25), his words are 'spirit and ... life' (John 6:63). In the Synoptic Gospels, life is almost always viewed as being in the future: In Johannine and Pauline writing there is the future element, but resurrection life is also viewed as a present possession of the believer. We pass from death to life at conversion (1 John 3:14, John 5:24), and now our life is inseparable from Christ – to have him is to have life (1 John 5:11).

MILLENNIUM QUOTES

"There seems every likelihood that the culmination of 2000 years of Christian history will degenerate into little more than a marketing opportunity."

– J.G. Ballard in *The Observer*

"I think of the television and of lots of parties. I also think of the millennium song that Robbie Williams did. I think that the millennium is something to do with Jesus."

– Danielle Jordan (8), Chaddesden

"I think of computers – there will be a lot of problems. I've heard about the Millennium Bug. It's the anniversary of Jesus' birth too – we were talking about it at school."

– Liam Firth (11), Mackworth

"It means the celebration of a thousand years, the beginning of a new century, the song Millennium and the Millennium Bug. I will be going to the Millennium Dome."

– Tom Middleton (10), Chaddesden

"I think of the Bug. If a computer is broken it is sent away to be mended. Also the song by Robbie Williams. I go to church and know that it's about Jesus' birthday."

– Jake Plunkett (5), Heanor

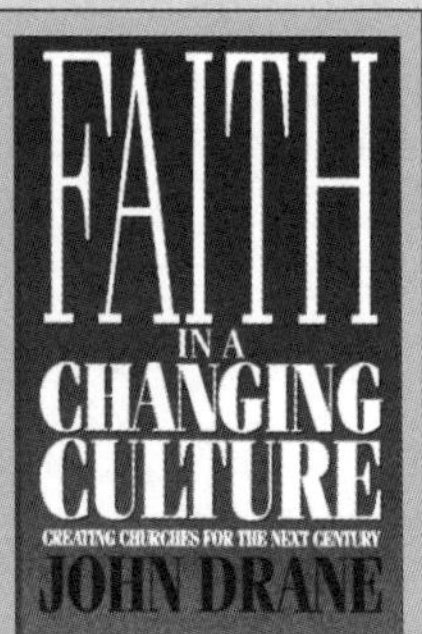

Faith in a Changing Culture – John Drane, Marshall Pickering

"Viagra is to be given a place of honour in the Millennium Dome. Christianity will be relegated to a portion of the Spirit Zone. That tells you all you need to know about today's sense of priorities. I shall not be visiting the wretched exhibition."

– Ann Widdecombe, Yorkshire Post, *3 July 1999*

The Divine Conspiracy – Dallas Willard, Fount

The Jesus I Never Knew – Philip Yancey, Marshall Pickering

millennium. The occasion was chaired by an executive from a TV company, and included people from all walks of life in Scotland: education, industry, finance, commerce, as well as government.

"Not a single person mentioned – not even vaguely or in passing – the fact that these 2000 years are counted from the time when Jesus Christ was born.

"After about 40 minutes of brainstorming, I eventually threw this observation into the discussion. Predictably, perhaps, it was a conversation-stopper – at least for 20 or 30 seconds. Two things were obvious: first, that those present already knew that it would be the 2000th anniversary of the birth of Jesus. But even with the best will in the world these people (who were not anti-Christian, and some of whom were church members) could not really see how that fact would have much relevance for the task of inspiring and equipping people for life in the new century."

Some politicians and national leaders argued that Jesus should feature clearly in the millennial celebrations. Sir Terence Conran, consultant to the Dome, has said however that it would be 'absolutely inappropriate' for the Dome to have a strong Christian or religious theme. Anne Widdecombe was planning to boycott the exhibition.

'I am the bread of life,' says Jesus – the very stuff of which real life is made. But there is a perception in our culture that the Church is irrelevant – and therefore, by association, Jesus is irrelevant.

Many people in Britain today view Jesus as a vague hero, a good, nice man, but little more. A few years ago, *Self* magazine polled its readers to determine the most popular personal public heroes. Jesus made the list, but he came in behind Mother Teresa, George Bush, Madonna, Norman Schwartzkopf, and Cher – tying with the Desert Storm Troops and Julia Roberts.

Uninvited by some academics

And some contemporary academics, in their search for the real or 'historical' Jesus, have succeeded in making Jesus seem all the more distant and out of touch.

Prolific writer and broadcaster A.N. Wilson claims that Jesus was nothing more than a simple Galilean holy man, a disappointing, mildly interesting figure, who was scarcely worth worrying about then nor is now. For Wilson, Jesus was not born of a virgin, he is no

JESUS DISREGARDED

"Very few people today find Jesus interesting as a person or of vital relevance to the course of their actual lives. He is not generally regarded as a real-life personality who deals with real-life issues but is thought to be concerned with some feathery realm other than the one we must deal with, and must deal with now. And frankly, he is not taken to be a person of much ability." – Dallas Willard

HAGUE'S VIEW

William Hague has backed the Church of England's call for prayers in the Millennium Dome and warned against events which would seem 'flimsy and irrelevant' to people 30 or 40 years from now.

In an interview with The Church of England Newspaper he stressed that there must be solemn moments amid the partying, adding that he was amazed the issue was still unresolved. He said: "The millennium is about Christ. That is what it is. It is the 2000th anniversary of the birth of Christ. That is what we are celebrating. Here we are, a predominantly Christian country – we should not be ashamed of celebrating the millennium with prayer. And I think that there should be, amid all the partying, some solemn moments."

NO ROOM AT THE MILLENNIUM DOME FOR JESUS, CONSULTANT CONRAN SAYS

"No 'Happy-Clappy' Evangelicals Wanted," by Barbie Dutter

A dominant Christian theme in the Millennium Dome would be "absolutely inappropriate," Sir Terence Conran, one of its creative consultants, said yesterday. The worst outcome would be a dome turned over to a "happy-clappy" evangelistic approach from which a Billy Graham figure would emerge, Sir Terence said. He said time, rather than religion, was the fundamental issue. "It is a millennium celebration, it is not an event that has very much to do with Christianity. It's to do with time," he said. "The birth date of Christ is unproven."

Sir Terence's comments will fuel the argument over how integral a Christian theme should be to the dome's content. Leading church figures say that the dome is, in part, a monument to Christianity as an acknowledgement that the millennium is a celebration of the birth of Jesus Christ.

Sir Terence, who has been consulted on numerous aspects of the exhibition, said he was "very, very doubtful" that the dome would have an overriding Christian or religious theme, adding: "It would be absolutely inappropriate if it did." – *The Daily Telegraph*

Who was Jesus? – NT Wright, SPCK

"If you peruse academic books at a seminary bookstore, you may encounter Jesus as a political revolutionary, as a magician who married Mary Magdalene, as a Galilean charismatic, a rabbi, a peasant Jewish Cynic, a Pharisee, an anti-Pharisee Essene, an eschatological prophet, a 'hippie in a world of Augustan yuppies', and as the hallucinogenic leader of a sacred mushroom cult. Serious scholars write these works, with little sign of embarrassment."

– *Philip Yancey,* The Jesus I Never Knew

The Jesus Quest – Ben Witherington III, Paternoster

The Radical Evangelical – Nigel Wright, SPCK

Messiah, or Second Person of the Trinity. James, the brother of Jesus, was wrongly mistaken for Jesus after the resurrection – hence the rumour (false, according to Wilson) that Jesus had been raised from the dead. For Wilson, Jesus was a moralist who would never have thought of founding a church and would even have considered the idea satanic! A leading evangelical scholar, N.T. Wright, describes Wilson's Jesus as 'a moderately pale Galilean.'

Barbara Thiering has proposed the notion that Jesus was married to Mary Magdalene, had three children – then he divorced and married again. Her provocative ideas have at least guaranteed her book *Jesus the Man: New Interpretation from the Dead Sea Scrolls* a large amount of publicity – and an entirely negative reaction from worldwide scholarship.

Bishop John Selby Spong has achieved a level of infamy recently, and in 1999 appeared on Melvyn Bragg's major television series, *Two Thousand Years*. As Bishop of Newark, New Jersey, he denies the literal, bodily resurrection of Jesus, and has announced that his crusade is to 'rescue the Bible from fundamentalism'. He sees Mary not as a virgin but as a victim of rape, and marries off Jesus to Mary Magdalene.

Uninvited by our lifestyle

As committed Christians we would be quick to affirm that Jesus is far more than a hero or distant holy man. We affirm without hesitation the reality that Christ is both human and divine.

But we must face a challenge. Is it possible that sometimes, in our eagerness to centre on his death and resurrection, we have forgotten Jesus' life? Were his thirty-three years prior to the cross just a supernaturally peppered preamble to Calvary. Was he just a man 'born to die' – or do we need to refocus our attention upon the life of Jesus? Did Jesus just come to 'arrange' to get us into heaven when we die – or to show us also in his life how we can live before death?

Nigel Wright points out that we can 'run the danger of losing the earthly Jesus in the heavenly Lord, or of regarding his life as merely the prelude to the saving work of the cross. Orthodox Christianity easily overlooks the historical Jesus and so downgrades the themes of discipleship and of imitation to Christ. Liberal Christianity helps restore the balance.'

BLURRED VISIONS?

H.S. Reimarus (1694–1768) saw Jesus as a Jewish revolutionary who died a failure. Christianity was, for Reimarus, an elaborate con – the disciples stole the body of Jesus, and Paul adapted their wild notions and spread them throughout the gullible ancient world. D.F. Strauss (1808–1874) amplified the scepticism of Reimarus and tried to deny any miraculous element to Christianity. F.E. Renan (1823–1892) painted a romantic portrait of Jesus as a popular teacher who began well but lost his popular appeal when his message became too demanding. For Renan, the message is still worth listening to even if, in his view, the Church has severely muddled it. Johannes Weiss (1863–1914) continued the suggestion that, to quote N.T. Wright, 'Jesus simply went about telling people to be nice to each other.'

Albert Schweitzer was just 30 years old when he wrote *The Quest of the Historical Jesus* in 1906. Initially it paints a historical backdrop in the quest for the historical Jesus. It then suggests that Jesus expected the end of the world within a very short time, and believed himself to be the Messiah – though not divine. Schweitzer's Jesus died a failure, betrayed by Judas, but his message lives on, as does his 'towering personality.' There are many other more contemporary portraits of Jesus – Jesus the wandering cynic preacher (Burton Mack and Dominic Crossnan), Jesus the merciful politician (Marcus Borg and Ed Sanders).

THE QUESTS

Quest 1 – Schweitzer's work was devastatingly influential. For the next 50 years or so, scholars largely abandoned the project of reconstructing Jesus' biography. A leading New Testament critic, Rudolph Bultmann, summed up the general mood when he declared we can know 'almost nothing about the life and personality of Jesus, since the early sources show no interest in either'. Ironically, it was one of Bultmann's students, Ernst Käsemann, who revived interest in the factual Jesus, and thereby initiated what came to be called the 'Second Quest'.

Quest 2 – Käsemann's work led him to suggest that the historical threads of Jesus' life were 'pitiful but not irrelevant'. Any historian worthy of the name would, he said, have to accept certain pieces of data as authentic. Operating from the same basic premise, Ernst Fuchs, Hans Conzelmann, Gunther Bornkamm and others proposed that painstaking analysis of early sources could present us with rough outlines of Jesus' real life.

Quest 3 – By the 1970s, extensive textual and archaeological discoveries were leading another group of scholars to focus more specifically on the Jewish background to the New Testament, and to explore Jesus' rabbinical and messianic identity. The so-called 'Third Quest' continues today, and includes a wide array of scholars, from Joachim Jeremias, Geza Vermes, E.P. Sanders and Marcus Borg to evangelicals like N.T. Wright and Ben Witherington III. More eccentric portraits have been produced by John Dominic Crossan (*Jesus as Social Revolutionary*) and Barbara Thiering (*Jesus and the Riddle of the Dead Sea Scrolls: Unlocking the Secrets of his Life Story*), among others.

Much of the work currently being done in 'Jesus Studies' can seem shocking to those who read the gospel accounts of Jesus' life at face-value. The US-based Jesus Seminar, for example, recently declared 80 per cent of the sayings attributed to Jesus in the New Testament to be inauthentic. Even so, the general recovery of confidence in the historical basis of Christianity does provide scope for classical, orthodox Christians to demonstrate that 'fact' and 'faith' are interdependent rather than mutually exclusive.

SECTION I
JESUS AT THE CENTRE

"To be a Christian is to be like Jesus Christ."

– Bishop Stephen Neill

"You and I are called to be persons after the manner of Jesus. Nothing else matters. Our goal is to become as Christ, to always have his image before our eyes. Søren Kierkegaard once described two types of Christians. Those who imitate Jesus Christ, and those who are content to speak about him."

– Brennan Manning

The Challenge of Jesus
– NT Wright, SPCK

www.nicene.com

Jesus, where is your life … – in the creed?

Vital through many centuries of Church history, the creed has provided the learned and illiterate alike with a distilled theology of the three persons of the Trinity. Generations of believers have memorised this summary of belief about God the Father, God the Son and God the Holy Spirit.

The Nicene Creed was adopted by the Church Council at Nicæa in AD 325 and appears in its present form by the Council at Chalcedon in AD 451. It has remained in use since that time.

We believe in one God, the Father, the Almighty,
maker of heaven and earth, of all that is, seen and unseen.

We believe in one Lord, Jesus Christ,
the only Son of God,
eternally begotten of the Father,
God from God, Light from Light,
true God from true God,
begotten, not made,
of one Being with the Father;
through him all things were made.
For us and for our salvation he came down from heaven;
by the power of the Holy Spirit he became incarnate of the Virgin Mary,
and was made man.
For our sake he was crucified under Pontius Pilate;
he suffered death and was buried.
On the third day he rose again
in accordance with the Scriptures;
he ascended into heaven
and is seated at the right hand of the Father.
He will come again in glory to judge the living and the dead,
and his kingdom will have no end.

We believe in the Holy Spirit,
the Lord, the giver of life,
who proceeds from the Father and the Son.
With the Father and the Son he is worshipped and glorified.
He has spoken through the prophets.

We believe in one holy catholic and apostolic Church.
We acknowledge one baptism for the forgiveness of sins.
We look for the resurrection of the dead,

LIBERAL CULS-DE-SAC?

Until the 18th century, virtually all theologians assumed a clear continuity between the historical man Jesus of Nazareth and the Jesus proclaimed as God in the creeds of the Church.

Likewise, they accepted that while the four Gospels offered different perspectives on Jesus, they could be integrated to form an accurate account of his life.

On this basis, scholars from Tatian in the second century to John Calvin in the 16th century produced 'harmonies' of the Gospels, which were widely distributed and used. Things began to change, however, with the onset of the Enlightenment. This was the period of scientific and philosophical exploration that inspired the American and French Revolutions of 1776 and 1789. Just as these two events produced a decisive separation of church and state, so the Enlightenment subjected divine revelation to the judgement of human reason. 'Supernatural' elements in the biblical record were radically questioned, and Jesus' incarnation, virgin birth, miracles and resurrection were called into doubt.

Herman Samuel Reimarus did much to define this new mood of scepticism. A professor of Oriental languages in Hamburg, Reimarus published *The Intentions of Jesus and his Teaching* in 1778. In this book, Reimarus argued that the apostles had embellished Jesus' original teaching, and had transformed him from a Jewish moral teacher into a cosmic redeemer. The idea of Jesus as a suffering saviour was, he wrote, invented to cover for an ultimately failed mission. What is more, Reimarus proposed that instead of rising from the dead, Jesus' body had been stolen from the tomb by the disciples. Reimarus was convinced that new insights from scientific and historical research would reveal the 'original' Jesus and so make these distinctions plain.

Reimarus is generally seen as the pioneer of what another German scholar, Albert Schweitzer, would later call *The Quest of the Historical Jesus*. This quest was taken up influentially by David Strauss. Strauss' *Life of Jesus* (1836) reinforced Reimarus' division of historical fact from supernatural 'fiction', although he conceded that the intentions of the apostles in mythologising the life of their leader were devotional rather than fraudulent. Strauss' work was translated into English by the novelist George Eliot, and became a key text in the development of liberal theology through the Victorian period. By the end of this period many scholars had come to take for granted Strauss' famous division between the 'Jesus of History' and the 'Christ of Faith'.

Albert Schweitzer acknowledged a considerable debt to Strauss, but after extensive research became far less optimistic about recovering the authentic Jesus. Rather than offering an unadorned, factual biography of Christ, he concluded that every account of him was inevitably distorted by the presuppositions of the author. Schweitzer was particularly hard on liberal theologians, who had, he said, constructed a liberal paragon in their own image, when Jesus was probably more concerned with the end of the world than with moral teaching. Schweitzer's Jesus is therefore a Jesus who comes to us 'as one unknown, without a name, as of old, by the lakeside, he came to those men who knew him not'. His significance is not as an historical figure, but as one who is 'spiritually risen within men' (*The Quest of the Historical Jesus*, 1906). This view has more recently been expressed by a former bishop of Durham, David Jenkins.

The Human Christ – Charlotte Allen, Lion

and the life of the world to come. Amen.

The life of Jesus is summed up as follows:

For us and for our salvation he came down from heaven;
by the power of the Holy Spirit he became incarnate of the Virgin Mary,
and was made man.
For our sake he was crucified…

The creed declares:

- The virgin birth of Jesus.
- The humanity of Jesus.
- The death of Jesus.

Jesus: Life or Legend? – Carsten Theide, Lion

The creed says quite a lot about Jesus, but what it does not say is just as important. It affirms that he is both divine and human but manages to ignore everything important about his human life, moving straight from his birth to his death. Where are his miracles, his relationships, his example, his teachings, his lifestyle? The creed affirms the divinity of Jesus and a belief that Jesus was also human, but does not affirm the reality of that human life. Though the creeds insist on his humanity, this seems little more than an abstract philosophical principle, unconnected to his way of life, relationships, teaching and miracles. The Jesus of the creed is an exalted figure, remote and powerful, but no longer disturbing the *status quo*.

The Original Jesus – NT Wright, Lion

Jesus, where is your life … – in the popular 'gospel' message?

There is a popular form of evangelistic preaching that presents good news about what is available through Christ, but sometimes the message focuses more on the benefits of being in Christ rather than the invitation to walk with Jesus himself – a kind of depersonalised 'Good Friday' agreement, a legal deal to be struck rather than a warm relationship to enjoy; an insurance policy rather than a person with whom we can share a close relationship.

The good news of the gospel should be centred in a person – Jesus – rather than a set of propositions about a person.

The Spirit of the Disciplines – Dallas Willard, Hodder & Stoughton

Jesus, where is your life … – in the Church?

If we are genuinely living out the Christian life, could we not expect to have a greater effect upon our culture? With very little resources, the Early Church had a dynamic effect upon their communities. Was this just because of their ability to be a supernatural church – or did

CREED AT SPEED

"The Creed hustles through Jesus' life in one paragraph, beginning with his birth and skipping immediately to his death, descent into hell, and ascent into heaven. Wait a minute – isn't something missing? What happened in the interval between his being born of the Virgin Mary and his suffering under Pontius Pilate? Somehow everything Jesus said and did in thirty-three years on earth gets swept aside in the rush to interpret his life. How did he spend his time here?" – *Philip Yancey*

OTHER VIEWPOINTS

Stuart Murray says, "The Nicene Creed was the result of a conference at Nicæa in AD 325 chaired by Emperor Constantine, whose main concern was not theology but having a united church in his empire."

Some would argue, however, that the creed doesn't focus on the theology of Jesus because that was not the issue at stake. Nicæa was convened to discuss the divinity of Christ and affirmed the Son was the same nature as the Father.

MENTAL ASSENT?

"Most conservatives by the early '70s generally accepted that being a Christian had nothing essentially to do with actually following or being like Jesus. It was readily admitted that most 'Christians' did not really follow him and were not really like him. 'Christians aren't perfect, just forgiven' became a popular bumper sticker. (While correct in the letter, this statement nullifies serious effort towards spiritual growth.) The only absolute requirement for being a Christian was that one believes the proper things about Jesus. The doctrinal struggles of many centuries had transformed saving faith into mere mental assent to correct doctrine." – *Dallas Willard*

Further Reading: Mark Allan Powell, *The Jesus Debate*. Oxford: Lion, 1998. Michael J. Wilkins & J.P. Moreland, *Jesus Under Fire: Modern Scholarship Reinvents the Historical Jesus*. Carlisle: Paternoster, 1996.

"If we preferred to be faithful rather than successful, the walls of indifference to Jesus Christ would crumble. A handful of us could be ignored by society; but hundreds, thousands, millions of such servants would overwhelm the world. Christians filled with the authenticity, commitment, and generosity of Jesus would be the most spectacular sign in the history of the human race. The call of Jesus is revolutionary. If we implemented it, we would change the world in a few months."

– Brennan Manning

book .link

Jesus – His Life and Ministry – Derek Prime, Word

book .link

How to Reach Secular People – George Hunter III, Abingdon

"An historian is a prophet in reverse."

– Friedrich von Schlegel, Das Athanaum

it also have something to do with the calibre and character of their faith and commitment to Christ?

More than a quarter of the population of the USA claim to be Christian. Some figures suggest that 34 per cent of the population profess a rebirth experience, others indicate that as many as 74 per cent have 'made a commitment to Christ.'

If such a large group of people are truly 'Christian', then could we not expect a massive influence for good and for God from them?

These challenges demand that we take a radical, searching look at the nature of what it means to be a Christian. Have we lost touch with the agenda of Christ, and settled for a 21st century version of Christianity that is a pale shadow of the real thing? Do we need to rediscover what it means to follow Jesus?

Is modern Christianity Christian?

Others have been brave enough to ask such a searching question.

George Hunter is Dean at Asbury Theological Seminary, Kentucky, USA. His examination of American Christianity has led him to describe much of what happens in the name of Christ as Christo-pagan – American civil religion in Christian clothing, 'a hash of moralism, patriotism, materialism, quests for the perfect high, celebrity-based wisdom mixed with selected Bible verses.'

Dietrich Bonhoeffer wrestled with these issues while held in a concentration camp. In April 1944, a year before his death, he wrote: "What is bothering me incessantly is the question of what Christianity really is, or indeed what Christ really is for us today."

How did we get here?

To appreciate how we developed our current understanding of what it means to be a Christian, we need to look back and take a trip through time to one of the most significant and formative moments of the Christian faith. Popular writer Philip Yancey and historian Dr. Stuart Murray agree – something went very wrong around 1,650 years ago.

The first 300 years

The infant Church was faced with the huge challenge of reaching a totally pagan, pre-Christian culture.

CHRISTIAN AMERICA

"According to Gallup surveys, 94 per cent of Americans believe in God and 74 per cent claim to have made a commitment to Jesus Christ. About 34 per cent confess to a 'new birth' experience. These figures are shocking when thoughtfully compared to statistics on the same group for unethical behaviour, crime, mental distress and disorder, family failures, addictions, financial misdealing, and the like.

"Of course there are always shining exceptions. But could such a combination of profession and failure really be the 'life and life abundantly' that Jesus said he came to give? Or have we somehow developed an understanding of commitment to Jesus Christ that does not break through to his living presence in our lives? Without question, it is the latter that has occurred, and with heart-rending consequences.

"Multitudes are now turning to Christ in all parts of the world. How unbearably tragic it would be, though, if the millions of Asia, South America and Africa were led to believe that the best we can hope for from the way of Christ is the level of Christianity visible in Europe and America today – a level that has left us tottering on the edge of world destruction." – *Dallas Willard*

A GOOD START

"The Early Church began well, placing a high premium on moral purity. Baptismal candidates had to undergo long periods of instruction, and church discipline was rigorously enforced. Sporadic persecution by Roman emperors helped to purge the Church of 'lukewarm' Christians, yet even pagan observers were attracted to the way Christians reached out to others by caring for the oppressed and devoting themselves to sick and the poor." – *Philip Yancey*

- **They had to face ignorance** – the story of Jesus had to be told carefully and clearly.
- **They had to face persecution** – the friendship of hostile people had to be won. Christians had lost their own lives caring for the sick and dying during a major outbreak of plague.
- **They had to offer choices** – there were several entrenched religions already in the empire and the Church called people to voluntary discipleship.
- **Then something happened that changed everything** – the emperor became a convert to Christianity.

In AD 312, there were two claimants to the imperial throne. Maxentius held the capital, Rome, and most of Italy, but Constantine held most of the western empire and had marched on Rome. In October 312, he was camped north of the city preparing for what would be the showdown with his rival, but worried because he did not have the resources for a long siege. Then something unusual happened.

book.link

Following Jesus – NT Wright, SPCK

According to both Christian and pagan writers of the time, Constantine had a vision in which he saw the sign of the cross with the sun rising behind it, and saw or heard the words "In this sign conquer." In response, Constantine had the sign of the cross painted on his soldiers' equipment – and won the ensuing battle. Convinced that the God of the Christians had helped him, he declared himself to be a Christian and 'converted' the Roman Empire.

The emperor and Jesus

In the following decades it seemed like revival – massive church growth, wonderful new church buildings, changes in laws and customs, church leaders taking on political and social roles, Constantine ruling as a Christian emperor. By the end of the century, Christianity had become the state religion, the only legal religion, and it was pagans who were being persecuted. The system known as Christendom was coming into being, an alliance between church and state that would dominate Europe for over 1000 years and which still impacts the way Christians think and act.

Two opposite assessments have been made of what happened in the fourth century:

This was a God-given opportunity which the Church rightly seized and which ensured the triumph of the Church and of Christianity in Europe;

CHURCH AND STATE

The basis of the Constantinian system was a close partnership between the Church and the state. The form of this partnership might vary, with either partner dominant or with a balance of power existing between them. There are examples from the fourth century onwards both of emperors presiding over church councils and of emperors doing penance imposed by bishops.

Throughout the medieval period, power struggles between popes and emperors resulted in one or other holding sway for a time. But the Christendom system assumed that the Church was associated with the Christian status quo and had vested interests in its maintenance. The Church provided religious legitimation for state activities, and the state provided secular force to back up ecclesiastical decisions.

Supporters of Christendom have argued that this system enabled the lordship of Christ to be exercised over every aspect of society and that it demonstrated the triumph of the gospel. Enthusiastic church leaders spoke of the fulfilment of the Great Commission and of the arrival of the millennium. This was the basis for the Early Church historian, Eusebius, to give his approval of Constantine, whose biography he wrote.

This was a disaster that perverted the Church, compromised its calling and hindered its mission, achieving through infiltration what 300 years of persecution had failed to achieve. That this was not the triumph of church over empire, but the triumph of empire over church.

Christendom meant:

- the adoption of Christianity as the official religion of city, state or empire;
- the assumption that all citizens (except for Jews) were Christian by birth;
- the imposition of a supposedly Christian morality on the entire population (although normally Old Testament moral standards were applied);
- a generic distinction between clergy and laity, and the relegation of the laity to a largely passive role.

Rather than society being sanctified, the Church was secularised. Constantinian thinking seems to have no place for elements of a New Testament vision such as:

- believers' churches composed only of voluntary members;
- a clear distinction between 'church' and 'world';
- evangelism and mission (except through military conquest of, or missions to, 'heathen' nations);
- a prophetic role in society – abandoned by the Church in favour of a role that is primarily priestly, providing spiritual support for groups and individuals and sanctifying social occasions and state policies;
- speaking out about social justice, the Church instead being primarily concerned with social order;
- mercy, with persecution imposed by those claiming to be Christian rather than upon them.

However this arrangement is evaluated, for three-quarters of its history the Church in Western Europe has operated within a Christendom framework. Only in the first three centuries, in persecuted dissident movements between the fourth and 16th centuries, and in the last five centuries, has this mindset been challenged. Constantinian thinking has influenced every aspect of theology and biblical interpretation.

The primary result of Constantinian thinking: the marginalising of Jesus

VOTING AGAINST THE EMPEROR

"A major change took place when the Emperor Constantine first legalized Christianity and made it a state subsidized religion. At the time his reign appeared to be the faith's greatest triumph, for the emperor was now using state funds to build churches and sponsor theological conferences rather than to persecute Christians. Alas, the triumph did not come without cost: the two kingdoms got confused. The state began appointing bishops and other church offices, and soon a hierarchy grew up that neatly replicated the hierarchy of the empire itself. As for their part, Christian bishops began imposing morality on society at large, not just the Church. I realize, as I look at the life of Jesus, how far we have come from the divine balance he set out for us. Listening to the sermons and reading the writings of the contemporary church in the United States, I sometimes detect more of Constantine than of Jesus." – *Philip Yancey*

Stuart Murray of Spurgeon's College agrees with Yancey:

"Constantine's Roman Empire was in turmoil. After centuries of dominance, the empire was showing signs of age – the bureaucracy was creaking, moral standards were low, the old forms of religion seemed empty, barbarians were attacking the frontiers. Despite almost 300 years of persecution, and despite still being an illegal society, the Church was one of the few remaining stabilising and civilising influences. Their sacrificial care for victims during a recent outbreak of plague had won them many admirers, even if their convictions still seemed strange. And then, suddenly, Emperor Constantine became a Christian believer.

"Historians have argued for centuries about whether Constantine was genuinely converted, but what is certain is that he saw Christianity as a force that could unite and revive his crumbling empire. The persecution ended, Christianity became a legal religion and Constantine invited church leaders to assist him in making the Roman Empire a Christian society."

VOTING FOR THE EMPEROR

Abraham Kuyper (quoted in *Leonard Verduin: Anatomy of a Hybrid* pp101–102) is positive about Constantine's actions: "When the first contest eventuated in this that the emperor bowed to Jesus, then ... the kingship of Christ began to be triumphant in society... . The kingship of Christ from this time on stood as a direction-giving power above the imperial power, which, in order to strengthen its influence, tried for an ever-increasingly close integration with the kingship of Jesus... . When in the fourth century persecution ceased and the imperial power evinced a readiness to accommodate itself to Jesus, the basic victory became apparent... . This principal victory continued on during the entire course of the long period known as the Middle Ages."

Others have suggested that the Church had no option in the fourth century but to accept imperial endorsement, and that Christendom, despite its excesses, was a providential means of Christianising culture and advancing God's kingdom.

Lesslie Newbigin has concluded (*The Other Side of 1984* p34): "How else, at that moment of history, could the Church have expressed its faithfulness to the gospel, which is a message about the universal reign of God? It is hard to see what other possibility there was at that moment. The experiment of a Christian political order had to be made."

The price to pay for Christendom was the marginalising of Jesus. This is always the price the Church pays when it tries to assume power. And make no mistake – in the fourth century Jesus was marginalised.

Furthermore, some of Jesus' teaching was difficult to apply in this new situation: How does a Christian emperor love his enemies? How can a Christian politician 'take no thought for tomorrow'? The Sermon on the Mount especially presented problems: perhaps it should be interpreted as relevant only for interpersonal relationships rather than public life, or regarded as an unattainable ideal in this age? In time, such teachings were regarded as 'counsels of perfection' rather than guidelines for discipleship.

The dangerous memory of what Jesus said and did, his dealings with political and religious authorities, his championing of the poor and his criticism of injustice were not helpful in a situation where church leaders were becoming politicians and supporters of the *status quo*.

Somehow, the connection between the radical Jesus and fourth century Christianity had to be loosened. A comparison of various documents at the beginning of the fourth century and the beginning of the fifth century reveals this change of focus. In the hymns the churches sang, in the sermons preached, in the teaching given to catechumens, as well as in theological treatises, Jesus and his teaching are given less and less attention. The Christ-centred focus of the New Testament writers and the early churches is replaced by a theological system in which the life of Jesus seems to be of marginal importance.

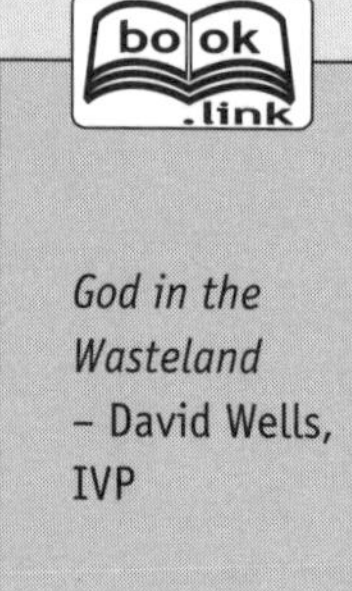

God in the Wasteland – David Wells, IVP

Of course, he was still honoured as Saviour and risen Lord, but the human Jesus (his example, lifestyle, teachings and relationships) was quietly ignored. He just did not fit the new arrangement, he was too awkward, too challenging, too threatening.

So, 2000 years later, we must stop and consider our understanding of what it means to be a Christian. What does it mean to walk in the life of God that John's gospel celebrates?

Banquet life

Life – full of God, full of peace, challenge, fulfilment. Let's take a look at the life that Jesus modelled for us – and how he helps us put it into practice.

DEVELOPING AN EMPIRE MODEL FOR THE CHURCH

Church leaders under Christendom soon realised that the New Testament provided inadequate guidelines for organising the kind of sacral society or hierarchical church that was emerging, but they found many helpful structures in the Roman Empire and often justified their adoption by appealing to the Old Testament. The model of church that operated within Christendom seemed to its critics to be an Old Testament model. Their persistent calls for a restoration of New Testament models of church and discipleship expressed both their dissatisfaction with the way in which this model operated and disagreement as to its legitimacy.

SECTION I

JESUS AT THE CENTRE

The good life

Ask the average person in the street what they want from their brief stay on this planet, and they will usually answer – 'I'd like to be happy.'

Advertising places before the person who wants to be happy an array of experiences, products or ideas that promise to create that elusive sense of buoyant wellbeing called happiness – and a lot of what's on sale can be grouped under the general heading of 'the good life'.

Christians in a Consumer Society – John Benton, CFP

The good life – *The Matrix* or *The Truman Show*?

Film fans will recall *The Matrix* as a false, virtual-reality world everyone lived in. *The Truman Show* was a huge elaborate mock-up world in a gigantic television studio, presided over by a dark, Satan-like producer.

Is the good-life world created by advertising agencies a hoax, a multi-million pound virtual reality where possession is everything but satisfaction is nowhere to be found? According to Jesus it is.

"And do not set your heart on what you will eat or drink; do not worry about it. 30For the pagan world runs after all such things, and your Father knows that you need them. 31But seek his kingdom, and these things will be given to you as well."

– Luke 12:29–31

The real good life – as demonstrated by Jesus.

Jesus announced that he brought with him a new order of living – abundant life, or life to the full (John 10:10).

When he arrived on our planet, he came as a human being. He did not walk around the earth as 'God with human skin on' but rather 'having emptied himself' (Phil 2:7 RSV), he became a human being. Having known the riches of godhead eternally, he who was rich became poor in order that we in turn might become rich (2 Cor 8:9).

"Sell your possessions and give to the poor. Provide purses for yourselves that will not wear out, a treasure in heaven that will not be exhausted, where no thief comes near and no moth destroys. 34For where your treasure is, there your heart will be also."

– Luke 12:33,34

The doctrine of the incarnation is incredibly complex, and we typically struggle with the idea of Jesus being fully human. Perhaps in our desire to defend the great doctrine of the divinity of Christ from liberal incursion we lose sight of the equally magnificent truth of his humanness. But if we are to learn from the rhythm and disciplines of Jesus' life, we must reaffirm that he lived a human life.

"... though he was rich, yet for your sakes he became poor, so that you through his poverty might become rich."

– 2 Cor 8:9

The human life modelled by Jesus is a life lived arm in arm with the Father, in an ongoing relationship and communion (John 14:10). The disciple he loved leans on Jesus (John 13:25). This good life is about dwelling or abiding in God (John 15:4–5).

The result of that ongoing communion and everyday spirituality

THE GOOD LIFE

Contemporary Westerners are nurtured on the faith that everyone has the right to do what they want when they want, to pursue happiness in all ways possible, to feel good, and to lead a 'productive and successful life', understood largely in terms of contentment and material well-being. This vision of life has come, in the popular mind, to be identified with 'the good life', and even with civilised existence. It is taught through the popular media, political rhetoric, and the educational system as the natural way for life to be.

Our commercialised environment takes this idea a step too far at times, frequently degrading the vision to its lowest possible level. An advertisement for an expensive car that ran for a long while in the papers urged readers to 'Pursue happiness in a car that can catch it!' In another paper there was a full-page advertisement for a certain brandy captioned: 'Taste the Good Life!' In Los Angeles a paper is published under the name *The Good Life*. From the contents one sees that the good life has to do exclusively with weight loss, eating (paradoxically), hairstyling, entertainment, celebrities, fancy cars. That's about it. These aptly characterise the giddy condition of much of our public life and private thinking. If for any reason we are not fully exercising and enjoying the right to 'freedom' and 'happiness' as popularly conceived, then we automatically assume that something is wrong. Either we have failed or circumstances (or other people) have treated us unfairly. If we ourselves refuse to work for this 'happy and successful life', we may be quickly dismissed as not wholly sane and rational – or worse still, written off as 'a saint'. The good life of advertisements is eating a chocolate bar on a sun kissed beach in paradise. It's being two stone lighter, or looking twenty years younger. It's what you wear, or what you have. It's the holiday of a lifetime, the feel of an expensive luxury car, or a sip of an exclusive brandy. It's owning a dream cottage in the country. This 'good life' is a hotchpotch of hedonism (just do it), escapism (the holiday location always looks better in the brochure), and materialism (shop till you drop).

More money is currently spent on advertising than on education, so in terms of influence advertising executives are our primary educators. They are successful, and therefore highly paid, teachers. We trust their message – and go out and buy their stuff. Millions of us are working harder, longer hours as we chase their good life. – *Dallas Willard*

WHOSE LIFE IS IT ANYWAY?

The Matrix is one of those films that Christians discussed with excitement when it was first released. The special effects spectacular, starring Keanu Reeves, is based around a clever storyline which many Christians saw as a modern day parable. *The Matrix* is a computer generated, virtual reality world in which all of humanity lives and interacts – but they were completely unaware of it. The real world has been taken over and devastated by raiding aliens. In order to control humanity, they have everyone living in this new reality, which is really of course a deception, a myth. Keanu Reeves attempts to liberate humanity from the false worldview – and, saviour-like, dies in the attempt and is reborn.

The Truman Show, starring Jim Carrey, tells the story of a baby born to star in a 24-hour, 7-day-a-week show centred around his life. He grows up and marries completely unaware of the hidden cameras, and more significantly, totally oblivious to the fact that everybody in his life is an actor, his world is a stage. There is a poignant scene at the end of the film, when Truman bumps into the edge of his world. Climbing some steps, he approaches a door that will lead him into the true, real world. The producer pleads with him: "There's no more truth out there than there is in the world I created for you. Same lies. Same deceit. But in my world you have nothing to fear. You can't leave, Truman, you belong here. With me." Does Truman continue to live in a virtual world of deception – or go through the door into the reality that awaits him? Rent the film and find out.

"A life lived for God is remarkably well rounded. Its joys are genuine, its peace profound, its humility deep, its power formidable, its love enveloping, its simplicity that of a trusting child. It is the life and power in which the prophets and apostles moved. It is the life and power of Jesus of Nazareth who taught that when the eye is single, the whole body is full of light."

– Thomas R. Kelly

book link

If Only …
– Nick Pollard, Hodder & Stoughton

"Holy people must stop going into 'church work' as their natural course of action and take up holy orders in farming, industry, law, education, banking, and journalism with the same zeal previously given to evangelism and missionary work."

– Dallas Willard

"He is, therefore, the devout person … who considers God in everything … who makes all the parts of his common life parts of piety, by doing everything in the name of God."

– William Law

was a whole life plan.

Jesus did not divide life into 'spiritual' and 'unspiritual' boxes the way we sometimes do. Partying with friends is presented alongside prayerful solitude – and the miraculous kissed both. Hugging children was of equal importance to theological debate with the Pharisees. In fact Jesus halted the debate in order for the giggling children to be gathered in his arms – much to the consternation of the disciples. They obviously wanted a more religious priority to prevail – an attitude that earned a rebuke from Jesus. Similarly, Jesus doesn't just 'do evangelism': it is seamlessly integrated into his life. Pausing for a drink and a rest at a well, he speaks a life changing message to a woman (John 4:7–26).

> **?** **A leader announced to the church, 'I know it's not very spiritual, but we have a church golf tournament this week.' Was he right about golf being unspiritual?**

So the good life we live, based on the Jesus model, will be:

- **A life with him in charge, and not life in charge of him.** Jesus freely expressed his emotions and desires – but he was not governed by them. He was a man in charge of himself, ruling over his body, emotions, and ambitions. He struggled in Gethsemane but remained obedient and faithful even in the horrifying shadow of the cross.

God wants us to be in authority over ourselves, reigning over our appetites and the demands of our bodies, rather than permitting them to reign over us. He gave us a spirit of self-discipline (2 Tim 1:7). Remember that we were created to rule on earth (Gen 1:28), we shall one day reign with Christ (Rom 8:17) and we will judge the world and the angels (1 Cor 6:3).

- **A life of growth and development.** Jesus learned obedience through suffering (Heb 5:8). He grew in wisdom and stature, as a pupil in life. In that sense Jesus himself was a disciple, a learner, an apprentice of the Father (John 7:16,17:8).
- **A life of rhythm and pace.** His was the most important agenda in the history of agendas! He had the message to proclaim, a somewhat slow-learning team to train, countless demands on his time from leaders who wanted to draw him into interroga-

JESUS THE EVERYDAY PERSON

A few years ago a Spring Harvest speaker caused great consternation in a few people by suggesting that Jesus, as a human being, would have had normal bodily functions and therefore would have gone to the toilet. This offended some people, who saw the idea as blasphemous. Dr. Stuart Murray has commented that we find it easier to think of Jesus sitting on a throne in heaven than to recognise that as a human being he would have squatted to have a bowel movement – a perfectly natural and God-created biological function. Our discomfort with these issues is rooted perhaps in normal social propriety, but is also tinged with a refusal to be at home with the reality that Jesus was human.

This is more important than we might first realise. Docetism – the idea that Jesus did not really come in the flesh, but that his physical body was an illusion – is a lingering heresy and an idea spawned by the spirit of antichrist. "Every spirit that acknowledges that Jesus Christ has come in the flesh is from God, [3]but every spirit that does not acknowledge Jesus is not from God. This is the spirit of the antichrist" (1 John 4:2,3).

FULLY HUMAN?

Do we believe the Christmas card portrayal of the Nativity – surreal looking individuals bedecked with halos, worshipping a Jesus who is sitting up on the knee of his mother despite being only 30 minutes old?

Do we believe the Christmas carol that affirms, 'But little Lord Jesus, no crying he makes' – as if Jesus were an extraterrestrial and the first baby who never cried? Crying is seen as somehow inappropriate to his status. John makes it perfectly clear that Jesus as an adult was in the habit of crying openly (John 11:35) – so why would he not have done the same as a baby?

JESUS AND THE FATHER

Jesus lived for God. The central theme in the personal life of Jesus of Nazareth is growing intimacy with, trust in, and love for his Father. His inner life was centred on God. The Father meant everything to him. "Father, the time has come. Glorify your Son, that your Son may glorify you" (John 17:1). The will of the Father was the air that he breathed. "The Son can do nothing by himself; he can do only what he sees his Father doing" (John 5:19). The Father's will was a river of life, a bloodstream from which he drew life more profoundly than from his mother. "For whoever does the will of my Father in heaven is my brother and sister and mother." (Matt 12:50) He lived secure in his Father's acceptance. "As the Father has loved me, so have I loved you" (John 15:9). – *Brennan Manning*

Destiny
– Matt Bird, Hodder & Stoughton

"Though I am always in haste, I am never in a hurry because I never undertake more work than I can go through with calmness of spirit."

– John Wesley

Work – Prison or Place of Destiny?
– David Oliver, Word

"Superficiality is the curse of our age."

– Richard Foster

tion and debate, sick people who needed healing and crowds who were like lost sheep without a shepherd. All this, and the work of redemption as well. But we never see him hurried, bowing to the demands of others (John 11:21) disorientated, or emotionally fractured by the pressure.

- **A life of destiny and purpose.** Resolutely refusing distraction, false opportunity and opposition, Jesus proceeded through his life to ultimately live out the single most significant existence that there has ever been – overcoming the whole world (John 16:33). We have an invitation to be 'history makers' in partnership with the Father. He chose us before the world was even created and he has prepared good works for us to do as part of his eternal plan (Eph 1:4).
- **A life of depth and strength.** Jesus was far more than a teacher of ideas. The quality of his life is demonstrated by its resilience in the face of huge pressure and pain. There is nothing superficial about him – he faces gigantic challenge with prayer and fellowship with his father (John 17:1).
- **A life of moral excellence.** He was the spotless lamb of God (John 1:29), qualified by his unblemished purity to atone for our sins. But his character did not exude the severe, self-consciously proud austerity of the Pharisees. His was a holiness held together by love, so much so that the nobodies of the day – women, children and so-called sinners – rushed to be near him (John 4, 8:1–11). His days were filled with friendship, love, laughter and tears.
- **A life for ever.** The ultimate 'good life' triumphed over humanity's final, common enemy – death itself. Not for Jesus a few short years littered with trinkets. His was a full, rich experience that ultimately led to the banquet where time will never be called – when we will drink wine with him in the fullness of the Father's kingdom. Eternal life with Jesus is far more than existence forever – it's a never-ending interaction and friendship with God.

No wonder that Jesus launches his ministry in John's gospel with the sign of the wine at Cana (John 2:1–11). This is the best quality, in overwhelming quantity. This is the good life!

? How can we apply these lessons from Jesus' good life to imitate him more closely?

NO HURRY

It is refreshing, and salutary, to study the poise and quietness of Christ. His task and responsibility might well have driven a man out of his mind. But he was never in a hurry, never impressed by numbers, never a slave of the clock. He was acting, he said, as he observed God to act – never in a hurry.

– *Phillips*, Your God is too Small

"Jesus came among us to show and teach the life for which we were made. By relying on his word and presence we are able to reintegrate the little realm that makes up our little life into the infinite rule of God. And this is the eternal kind of life. Caught up in his active rule, our deeds become an element in God's eternal history. They are what God and we do together, making us part of his life and him a part of ours. By taking the title 'son of man', he staked his claim to be all that the human being was originally supposed to be – and surely much more. Colloquially we might describe him as humanity's fair haired boy, the one who expresses its deepest nature and on whom its hopes rest. Older theologians soberly referred to him as 'the representative man' or the 'federal head' of humanity. The really good news for humanity is that Jesus is now taking students in the master class of life. The eternal life that begins with confidence in Jesus is a life in his present kingdom, now on earth and available to all. Eternity is now in flight and we with it, like it or not."

– Dallas Willard

Just Like Jesus – Max Lucado, Word

The Banquet Life 1

Jesus as life example – 'Follow me' (John 12:26)

As we hear the call of Jesus, 'follow me', we recognize again that:

- the human life of Jesus is vital and cannot be ignored.
- that Jesus is our model, our pioneer, our leader, our teacher, our example – as well as our redeemer.
- that he was truly human and that his humanity matters.
- that the awkward teachings of Jesus are relevant and authoritative in every area of life – in politics as much as in family life, in social policy as well as church life, in economics as well as personal morality.
- that the Sermon on the Mount is meant to be lived, not just admired.

Imitating Jesus

The words 'imitation' and 'image' have the same root, so that imitation of something or someone involves the reflecting of some or all of their attributes.

What does it mean to imitate Christ? To imitate someone is to copy his or her actions as closely as possible. It is to model our lives after the characteristics of someone we look up to.

Christians are encouraged to imitate Christ as part of the process of sanctification, so that their lives are a reflection or image of the life of Christ in his sonship of God and in his virtues, behaviour and intention. Imitation involves not simply the focus of spiritual and moral attention on the example of Christ, although this is important; it also implies the conforming or moulding of the life of the Christian, through grace, to the likeness of Christ.

Some areas where we are challenged to emulate Jesus would be in:

dependence
bravery and risk
loyalty to friends
serving others
responding to the poor
forgiving those who hurt us
resisting temptation
handling possessions.

One example of this desire to follow the model of Jesus in daily life is the What Would Jesus Do? (WWJD) movement. Young people

DON'T WEEP FOR ME, JOIN ME

"The Christ of the New Testament is not the God of the philosophers, speaking with detachment about the Supreme Being. We do not expect to find the Supreme Being with spit on his face. It jars us to discover that the invitation Jesus issues is: Don't weep for me; join me. The life I have planned for you is a Christian life, much like the life I led."
– *Brennan Manning*

DO AS I DO

Jesus said to his disciples: "You call me 'Teacher' and 'Lord,' and rightly so, for that is what I am. Now that I, your Lord and Teacher, have washed your feet, you also should wash one another's feet. I have set you an example that you should do as I have done for you." (John 13:13–15)

The apostle John wrote: "Whoever claims to live in him must walk as Jesus did" (1 John 2:6). In a letter to the Corinthians, Paul wrote: "Follow my example, as I follow the example of Christ" (1 Cor 11:1); and wrote to his friends at Philippi: "Your attitude should be the same as that of Christ Jesus" (Phil 2:5).

THE WAY JESUS DID IT

"Perhaps it is no wonder that the women were first at the cradle and last at the cross. They had never known a man like this – there had never been such another. A prophet and teacher who never nagged at them, who never flattered or coaxed or patronized; who never made arch jokes about them, never treated them either as 'The women, God help us!' or 'The ladies, God bless them!'; who rebuked without querulousness and praised without condescension; who took their questions and arguments seriously, who never mapped out their sphere for them, never urged them to be feminine or jeered at them for being female; who had no axe to grind and no uneasy male dignity to defend; who took them as he found them and was completely unselfconscious. There is no act, no sermon, no parable in the whole gospel that borrows its pungency from female perversity; nobody could possibly guess from the words of Jesus that there was anything 'funny' about woman's nature. But we might easily deduce it from his contemporaries, and from prophets before him, and from his Church to this day." – *Dorothy Sayers*

particularly are urged to wear wristbands with the initials WWJD prominently displayed as a prompt to make decisions that are consistent with what Jesus might be expected to do in a given situation. The founders of the movement started with a basic pre-supposition – if each person asked themselves 'What Would Jesus Do?' with each decision they made, the world would be changed for the better one question at a time.

Some have argued that the approach has limited effect, because it calls us to make crisis decisions to emulate Jesus rather than live continually in the transforming disciplines that cause us to be changed rather than simply conform to certain external behaviour patterns. At very least, the WWJD movement has promoted a greater consciousness of a Jesus-centred spirituality and morality.

Christians often talk about 'abiding in Christ' and 'practising the presence of God.' What does this mean in practical terms on a Monday morning?

WWW http//web link

www.wwjd.com

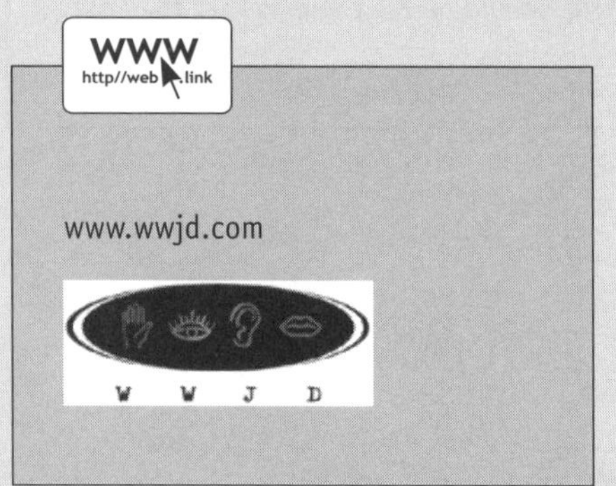

The Banquet Life 2

Jesus as life source – 'I am the vine' (John 15:5)

Jesus is more than our ethical example – we will never be able to live out his ethics if we don't experience his grace. It has been said that the Christian life is not difficult, it's impossible.

The Sermon on the Mount towers like a mountain over us if we don't have Jesus at our side, his power helping us to live out his teaching.

Christianity is not merely a moral code – Jesus is more than moral teacher and moral example – he lives his life in and through us. Jesus is emphatic: 'apart from me you can do nothing' **(John 15:5b)**.

This presents us with practical implications about:

Our spirituality – John's gospel carries the consistent theme of belief that leads to intimacy with God, which in turn leads to action. It has been suggested that evangelical Christianity is unappealing to some because it is insufficiently spiritual. We will be examining the spirituality of Jesus.

Our disciplines – have we rejected discipline, dismissing it as

WHAT WOULD JESUS DO?

The What Would Jesus Do? (WWJD) movement began when members of a youth group in Holland, Michigan, were inspired by a 19th century novel. It has grown into a raging fire, impacting millions worldwide as they ask the question, 'What Would Jesus Do?' Some 14 million wear a WWJD bracelet as a statement of their allegiance to this putative cultural revolution.

The youth group at Calvary Reformed Church pondered how to effect their generation. They studied Charles Sheldon's book *In His Steps* in which a tramp dressed in rags disrupts a church service.

'It seems to me, there's an awful lot of trouble in the world that somehow wouldn't exist if all the people who sing such songs went and lived them out,' the tramp says. With that, he dies. The congregation is stunned, and pledge to live for one year asking one question – What Would Jesus Do?

Like the congregation in the novel, the youth group was stunned. They too pledged to ask 'What Would Jesus Do?' and (to remind themselves) found someone to make woven bracelets that bore four letters – WWJD – representing the question. The bracelets led to many questions from friends, classmates, and parents. Soon, the community was wearing the bracelets, and it spread from there.

The organisers say: "At a time when values in education is a hot topic for schools, when the news is filled with reports of political corruption, moral failure, and the impact of greed on the lives of millions, these four letters make an impact on those who ask the question they represent – 'What Would Jesus Do?' The answer impacts the core values of the moral fabric of our society. Beyond sex-sexuality-sexual harassment all areas of decision are impacted – integrity, generosity, fairness, right or wrong choices, truth or lies, love or hate, racism, materialism. WWJD simply says, true love asks what would Jesus do in all things.

"WWJD stands in direct contrast to the 'just do it' mentality of advertisers, who encourage kids to enjoy life with no moral boundaries – justifying hedonistic and narcissistic passions with situation ethics framed as freedom of choice for lifestyles."

TIN MAN SYNDROME

"Our faith is not a matter of our hearing what Christ said long ago and trying to carry it out. The real Son of God is at your side. He is beginning to turn you into the same kind of thing as himself. He is beginning, so to speak, to 'inject' his kind of life and thought, his *zoe* [life], into you; beginning to turn the tin soldier into a live man. The part of you that does not like it is the part that is still tin."
– *C.S. Lewis*

empty legalism. How can the spiritual disciplines be a pathway to personal transformation? How can we rediscover what it means to be disciples of Jesus, the Church being God's discipling community? How did Jesus disciple?

Our evangelism – what kind of life are we inviting the world to embrace in our proclamation of the gospel?

The Banquet Life 3

Jesus as lens – 'I am the way' (John 14:6)

We have considered Jesus as our model and source of life. Finally, in our desire to put Jesus at the place of 'pre-eminence' (Col 1:16–18 John14:6) and centrality in our lives, we consider him as our 'lens' for life, seven days a week. We see him as the ultimate expression of God's revelation to us, and so we endeavour to develop a Jesus-centred view and interpretation on life including the way we view and interpret scripture.

"The Sermon on the Mount is not a set of principles to be obeyed apart from identification with Jesus Christ. The Sermon on the Mount is a statement of the life we will live when the Holy Spirit is getting his way with us."

– Oswald Chambers

? **It has been said that the Church would rather worship Jesus than follow him. Do you agree?**

? **If you start with Jesus to define your understanding of giving, is the practice of giving one-tenth radical enough?**

A Christocentric approach affects all kinds of issues. It profoundly challenges the way we worship, evangelise, work, treat creation, run our churches, get involved in society, exercise power, etc. It is urgent that we recover this approach. It was this approach that enabled the early churches to turn the world upside down. It was this that challenged their contemporaries and amazed their persecutors. It was this that was lost through the Christendom shift of Constantine. Christendom is dead, or dying.

We live in a post-Christian society and we desperately need to stop thinking in Christendom categories. Europe has rejected Christendom. Arguably it has not yet seen enough of Jesus to decide what to do with him.

The real Jesus is our trump card. The real Jesus is strangely attractive to people. Jesus is our central theme, the Church's best kept

JESUS AS VINE

If you were a first-century Jew and heard for the first time that Jesus was the true vine and his people were the branches (John 15:1,5), you would have mixed emotions. On one hand, you would be quite familiar with the idea of comparing people to vines and vineyards. Grapevines were a familiar sight in Palestine. Your Bible, the Old Testament, frequently refers to Israel as being a vine that God planted. You may have recited Psalm 80 in your morning prayers. In verses 8–9 the Psalmist says to God: "You brought a vine out of Egypt; you drove out the nations and planted it. You cleared the ground for it, and it took root and filled the land." You would know how God brought Israel out of Egypt and planted it in the promised land. You would have read the words of the Hebrew prophets who likened Israel to a vine or vineyard. You would recall the words of Hosea who said: "Israel was a spreading vine; he brought forth fruit for himself" (Hos 10:1). Hosea meant that Israel increased in prosperity. But he went on to say that Israel's prosperity unfortunately led to increased idolatry: As his fruit increased, he built more altars; as his land prospered, he adorned his sacred stones.

You may have chanted these words of Isaiah: "I will sing for the one I love a song about his vineyard: My loved one had a vineyard on a fertile hillside. He dug it up and cleared it of stones and planted it with the choicest vines. He built a watchtower in it and cut out a winepress as well. Then he looked for a crop of good grapes, but it yielded only bad fruit" (Isa 5:1–2). No doubt, you were haunted time and again with the words of God spoken to his people through Jeremiah: "I had planted you like a choice vine of sound and reliable stock. How then did you turn against me into a corrupt, wild vine?" (Jer 2:21). That would have reminded you of Ezekiel's chilling words spoken against Judah: "Therefore this is what the Sovereign LORD says: As I have given the wood of the vine among the trees of the forest as fuel for the fire, so will I treat the people living in Jerusalem" (Ezek 15:6).

You, as a first-century Jew, would be very familiar with the symbolic meaning of vine and vineyard. In fact, the idea was so prevalent in the first century that in one of his parables Jesus expressly made use of the vineyard motif as symbolism for Israel (Mark 12:1–12). Jesus concluded the parable by saying that the owner will destroy the tenants and give the vineyard to others. In response to the parable, the religious leaders wanted to arrest Jesus because (v.12) 'they knew he had spoken the parable against them.' The symbolism of vineyard was not lost on them.

However, just because you would be familiar with biblical references to vine and vineyard, that would not necessarily make it easy for you to understand how Jesus could be the true vine. For one thing, vine in the Old Testament always represented the whole people of Israel rather than a single individual. How could something that symbolized the whole people of Israel be a symbol of Jesus as an individual?

Secondly, whenever the Old Testament prophets, as well as the parable of Jesus mentioned above, made reference to vine or vineyard, they always had in mind the imminent judgment that God would bring upon his disobedient people. In other words, the idea of vine would not bring positive images to your mind. You would be reminded of vine twigs that are good for nothing but as firewood. For this reason, the gospel of John refers to Jesus not simply as the vine but more specifically as the true vine. The implication is that in contrast to Israel, which became unfaithful and incurred the judgment of God, Jesus remains faithful and thus fulfils Israel's calling to be the vine of God. It is noteworthy that the contrast is between Israel and Jesus, not between Israel and the Church. The Church is not the true vine; Jesus is. Furthermore, Jesus is not the trunk or the root; he is the vine. He is the true vine who fulfilled the destiny to which Israel was called. The Church can be a part of that destiny only as branches in the vine. The Church cannot fulfil Israel's destiny without Christ. Apart from Christ the Church is nothing but dead twigs.

– Jirair S. Tashjian

secret. In the words of Stuart Murray: "It is time to rediscover Jesus and to follow him into a world that is heartily sick of Christianity but which might yet fall in love with Jesus."

Jesus and Women

As we take a Christocentric approach to Scripture, we realize that what Jesus said and did, the way that he viewed and treated women are of primary importance.

As far as we can understand, he chooses to be born of a woman and place himself under her temporal authority.

Long conversations with women (eg John 4:4–42; Mark 5:33–34; Mark 7:24–30) even though this was not 'respectable' practice.

Jesus pronounces a new and radical responsibility for men in relation to them seeing women as sex objects (Matt 5:27–30), which went against the views of his day.

Equal rights – responsibilities in divorce (Mark 10:12).

Calls a woman a 'daughter of Abraham' (Luke 13:10–17) – not a term used of individuals.

Has women disciples – Mary is described as 'sitting at his feet' (Luke 10:39), a technical term for a disciple (Acts 22:3). Note also how Martha was fulfilling the more traditional 'women's role'.

Women are the first witnesses to the resurrection – even though their testimony would not have been valid in court, Jesus entrusts them with this most important function.

Jesus performed tasks that would have been seen as fulfilling traditionally female roles – cooking, washing feet and children sitting on knee.

In Christ the age to come broke – has broken – into the current age. How should that affect the relationships between men and women in church now? How should this influence our thinking about women in ministry and leadership?

"It is time to rediscover Jesus and to follow him into a world that is heartily sick of Christianity but which might yet fall in love with Jesus."

– Stuart Murray

book.link

Beyond Tithing – Stuart Murray, Paternoster

CHRISTOCENTRISM (CHRIST-CENTRED INTERPRETATION)

Christocentrism insists that Jesus is the centre of the Bible, the one to whom all the scriptures point, the one through whom all the scriptures must be interpreted. We do not start elsewhere and then try to fit in the teaching of Jesus (or ignore him if this is too awkward). We start with Jesus and interpret everything else in the light of what he models and teaches.

Jesus is the pinnacle of God's revelation:

Hebrews 1:1–2 "In the past God spoke to our ancestors through the prophets at many times and in various ways, but in these last days he has spoken to us by his Son, whom he appointed heir of all things, and through whom he made the universe".

Hebrews 12:2 "Looking at Jesus, the author and perfecter of our faith."

God has revealed himself in many ways, but in Jesus Christ he has provided the ultimate and definitive revelation. Jesus is the focal point, the central theme, the pinnacle of God's self-disclosure. He is central, not only for salvation, but for everything.

This does not mean that what God said previously is now obsolete, nor that God no longer speaks through prophets and in various ways in the past, or that he will not speak to us personally or prophetically in the future – but it does mean that every other revelation is tested against the ultimate revelation of God in Jesus Christ.

SOME CONTROVERSIAL EXAMPLES TO CONSIDER:

The status and role of women. Paul first or Jesus first? Do we interpret Jesus through Paul or Paul through Jesus? What does the way that Jesus empowered and honoured women have to say to us?

The status and role of tithing. Old Testament law first or Jesus first? Tithing was not practised until the Constantinian fourth century and was compulsory in Britain by legal act until 1936. Many say that it's a good starting point – but is it radical enough – or is it a compromise rooted in the Law rather than the radical giving example of Jesus?

SECTION I

JESUS AT THE CENTRE

SECTION 2

JESUS THE DISCIPLER

"The really good news for humanity is that Jesus is now taking students in the master class of life. The eternal life that begins with confidence in Jesus is a life in his present kingdom, now on earth and available to all."
– *Dallas Willard*

"Many of us have become as half-heartedly and conventionally religious as were the church folk of two thousand years ago, against whose mildness, mediocrity, and passionlessness Jesus Christ and his disciples flung themselves with all the passion of a glorious new discovery and with all the energy of builders of the kingdom of God on earth."
– *Thomas R. Kelly*

"The gospel will persuade no one unless it has so convicted us that we are transformed by it."
– *Brennan Manning*

"... the church has very efficiently pared the claws of the Lion of Judah, certified him as a fitting household pet for pale curates and pious old ladies ..."
– *Dorothy Sayers*

JESUS THE DISCIPLER

BIBLE PASSAGE

John 1:43–51

The next day Jesus decided to leave for Galilee. Finding Philip,
he said to him, "Follow me."

44 Philip, like Andrew and Peter, was from the town of Bethsaida.
45 Philip found Nathanael and told him, "We have found the one
Moses wrote about in the Law, and about whom the prophets
also wrote – Jesus of Nazareth, the son of Joseph."

46 "Nazareth! Can anything good come from there?" Nathanael
asked.

"Come and see," said Philip.

47 When Jesus saw Nathanael approaching, he said of him, "Here
is a true Israelite, in whom there is nothing false."

48 "How do you know me?" Nathanael asked.

Jesus answered, "I saw you while you were still under the fig
tree before Philip called you."

49 Then Nathanael declared, "Rabbi, you are the Son of God; you
are the King of Israel."

50 Jesus said, "You believe because I told you I saw you under the
fig tree. You shall see greater things than that." 51 He then added,
"I tell you the truth, you shall see heaven open, and the angels of
God ascending and descending on the Son of Man."

Comment

v43 The big invitation – 'follow me'

vv43–51 Philip and Nathaniel

Who were they?

And what did the invitation mean for them?

v48 The all knowing Christ

The disruption of discipleship

v43 changed priorities

v46 changed thinking and reversal of prejudices and preconceptions

v48 change of identity to one known by Christ

vv50,51 change of expectations from life 'you shall see greater things'

NOTES

JESUS THE DISCIPLER

I am the **true vine**, and my **Father** is the **gardener**. John 15:1

No **branch** can bear **fruit** by itself; it must remain in the **vine**.

Neither can you bear **fruit** unless you **remain** in **me**. John 15:4

I am the **vine**; you are the **branches**.

If a man **remains in me** and **I in him**, he will **bear** much **fruit**; apart from me you can do nothing. John 15:5

I chose you and appointed you to **go** and **bear fruit**—fruit that will **last**. John 15:16

I have **chosen** you out of the world.

That is why the world hates you. John 15:19

The one who **feeds on me** will live because of me. John 6:57

We are **one**:

I in them and

you in **me**. John 17:22

JESUS THE DISCIPLER – MENU

We've been focusing on the marvellous invitation that Jesus gives us to *The Royal Banquet.* A banquet is profoundly different from, say, an experience of eating at a fast-food franchise or inching your car through a drive-through hamburger outlet. The purpose of the latter is to get what you want – fast – and get moving again. The food is the important thing.

A banquet is a long, relational, carefully prepared experience. Fine food is hoped for, but the purpose of a banquet is the celebration of relationship. Friendship, laughter and conversation are the most important elements of the banquet event.

Jesus doesn't come as the fast food distributor of blessings – get saved, *fast,* and then hurry on with life as usual. Rather, he invites us to live a life in his company, a life centred on the one who blesses, and not just his blessing. This is the life of discipleship – the normal life for every Christian. It is a never-ending journey, arm in arm with the master.

THE GUEST

THE GUEST

Some material for this section has been adapted from an article by Dallas Willard in *Christianity Today*.

Discipleship – New Testament norm

The word 'disciple' occurs 269 times in the New Testament. 'Christian' is found three times, and was first introduced to refer precisely to the disciples in a situation where it was no longer possible to regard them as a sect of the Jews (Acts 11:26). The most common word used to describe someone who is committed to Jesus is 'disciple' (*mathetes*, literally, pupil/learner). A good translation might be 'apprentice' in that an apprentice is called to

- be with a mentor
- observe their skills
- emulate their mentor
- ultimately mentor others in the same skills.

"Most problems in contemporary churches can be explained by the fact that the members have not yet decided to follow Christ."

The New Testament is a book about disciples, by disciples, and for disciples of Jesus Christ. And the kind of life we see in the earliest Church is that of a special type of person. All the assurances and benefits offered to humankind in the gospel evidently presuppose such a life and do not make realistic sense apart from it.

The disciple of Jesus is not the deluxe or heavy-duty model of the Christian – specially padded, textured, streamlined and empowered for the fast lane on the straight and narrow way. The disciple stands on the pages of the New Testament as the first level of basic transportation in the kingdom of God.

The Spirit of the Disciplines – Dallas Willard, Hodder & Stoughton

The Lost Art of Disciple Making – Leroy Eims, Zondervan

Discipleship as an option

For at least several decades, Western churches have not made discipleship a condition of being a Christian. One is not required to be, nor to intend to be, a disciple to become a Christian, and one may remain a Christian without any signs of progress toward or in discipleship.

Discipleship then: going around with Jesus

When Jesus walked among humankind there was a certain simplicity to being his disciple. Primarily it meant to go with him, in an attitude of study, obedience and imitation. There were no correspondence courses. One knew what to do and what it would cost. Simon Peter exclaimed: "We have left everything to follow you!" (Mark 10:28). Family and occupations were deserted for long peri-

DISCIPLESHIP – OPTIONAL OR COMPULSORY?

Many churches do not require following Christ in his example, spirit, and teachings as a condition of membership – either of entering into or continuing in fellowship of a denomination or local church. So far as the visible Christian institutions of our day are concerned, discipleship clearly is optional.

That, of course, is no secret. The best of current literature on discipleship either states outright or assumes that a Christian may not be a disciple at all – even after a lifetime of being a church member. A widely used book, *The Lost Art of Disciple Making,* presents the Christian life on three possible levels – the convert, the disciple, and the worker. There is a process for bringing persons to each level, it states. Evangelising produces converts, establishing or follow-up produces disciples, and equipping produces workers. Disciples and workers are said to be able to renew the cycle by evangelising, while only workers can make disciples through follow-up.

But this kind of thinking gives the impression that discipleship is entirely optional. Vast numbers of converts today thus exercise the options permitted by the message they hear: they choose not to become – or at least do not choose to become – disciples of Jesus Christ. Churches are filled with 'undiscipled disciples' as Jess Moody has called them.

Little good results from insisting that Christ is supposed to be Lord: to present his lordship as an option leaves it squarely in the category of wide tyres and stereo equipment for a new car. You can do without it.

"It is enough for the student to be like his teacher."

– Matt 10:25

"... everyone who is fully trained will be like his teacher."

– Luke 6:40

ods to go with Jesus as he walked from place to place, announcing, showing and explaining the governance of God. Disciples had to be with him to learn how to do what he did.

Imagine doing that today. How would family members, employers, and co-workers react to such abandonment? Probably they would conclude that we did not much care for them, or even for ourselves. Did not Zebedee think this as he watched his two sons desert the family business to keep company with Jesus (Mark 1:20)? Ask any father in a similar situation. So when Jesus observed that one must forsake the dearest things – family and even his own life (Luke 14:26) – to accompany him, he stated a simple fact: it is the only possible doorway to discipleship.

I Believe in Discipleship – Rob Warner, Hodder & Stoughton

Discipleship now: more complex

Though costly, discipleship once had a very clear, straightforward meaning. **The mechanics are not the same today. We cannot literally be with him in the same way as his disciples could.** But the priorities and intentions – the heart or inner attitudes – of disciples are forever the same. In the heart of a disciple there is a desire and decision, or settled intent. Having come to some understanding of what it means and thus having counted up the costs, the disciple of Christ desires above all else to be like him.

"Holiness is a thousand decisions."

Discipleship is not optional – but it is still a choice

There is a decision to be made: the decision to devote oneself to becoming like Christ. The disciple is one who, intent upon becoming Christlike and so dwelling in his faith and practice, systematically and progressively rearranges his or her affairs to that end. By these actions, even today, one enrols in Christ's training, and becomes his pupil or disciple. There is no other way.

The Signature of Jesus – Brennan Manning

Discipleship is not a sad, bitter pill to be avoided

Not to follow Jesus is to lose life. Non-discipleship costs abiding peace, a life penetrated throughout by love, faith that sees everything in the light of God's overriding governance for good, hopefulness that stands firm in the most discouraging of circumstances, power to do what is right and withstand the forces of evil. In short it costs exactly that abundance of life that Jesus said he came to bring (John 10:10). The cross-shaped yoke of Christ is after all an instrument of liberation and power to those who live in it with him, and learn the meekness and lowliness of heart that brings rest to the soul.

ACCEPTING DISCIPLESHIP

A Polish Jew who survived the massacre of the Warsaw ghetto and later converted to Christianity discovered that on the acceptance or rejection of the crucified Lord hangs the meaning of discipleship:

"As I looked at that man upon the cross, I knew I must make up my mind once and for all, and either take my stand beside him and share in his undefeated faith in God or else fall finally into a bottomless pit of bitterness, hatred, and unutterable despair."

DECISIONS, DECISIONS

Following Jesus will be socially expensive. When the disciples decided to follow Jesus they "left everything" (Luke 5:11, 28). Jesus expects prospective disciples to sit down and calculate the cost of following him before they decide. They should follow only after completing a deliberate cost analysis otherwise they'll end up ridiculed, confused, and devastated.

No hocus-pocus is involved here. Disciples follow Jesus' way fully aware they may be embarrassed or lose a promotion. We deliberately love and serve even when this triggers ridicule and social harassment. Picking up the cross means we engage in an active basin ministry, knowing it may bring ostracism and rejection.

The number and kind of crosses depends on the social and political setting. The same act of love in one political context may bring frowns and gossip in another. It may bring imprisonment, torture or even death. Regardless of the shape or form of the cross, the disciple, following the example of Jesus, doesn't retaliate or seek revenge.

Cross-bearing isn't a one-time decision. It's a daily assessment of our willingness to make expensive decisions for the sake of Christ. Again and again, day after day, the call comes: "And anyone who does not carry his cross and follow me cannot be my disciple" (Luke 14:27), "and anyone who does not take his cross and follow me is not worthy of me" (Matt 10:38).

Following in the way of Jesus doesn't mean going barefoot, remaining celibate, or camping in rural areas. We follow him by engaging in basin ministries (serving) and accepting their concrete social consequences. We follow by making expensive decisions. – *Donald Kraybill*

THE COST OF DISCIPLESHIP

In 1937 Dietrich Bonhoeffer gave the world his book *The Cost of Discipleship*. It was a masterful attack on 'easy Christianity' or 'cheap grace', but it did not set aside – perhaps it even enforced – the view of discipleship as a costly spiritual excess and only for those especially driven or called to it. It was right to point out that one cannot be a disciple of Christ without forfeiting things normally sought in human life, and that one who pays little in the world's coinage to bear his name has reason to wonder where he or she stands with God. But the cost of non-discipleship is far greater – even when this life alone is considered – than the price paid to walk with Jesus.

JESUS THE DISCIPLER

"The Christian stands, not under the dictatorship of a legalistic 'You ought', but in the magnetic field of Christian freedom, under the empowering of the 'You may'."

– Helmut Thielicke

Discipleship is not perfection or 'working for your ticket'

Discipleship is not about perfection, nor about earning God's gift of life. It is concerned only with the way we enter into that life. While no-one can merit salvation, all must act if it is to be theirs. By what actions of the heart, what desires and intentions, do we find access to life in Christ?

Paul's example instructs us. He could say in one breath both 'not that I have already been made perfect' (Phil 3:12) and 'Whatever you have learned or received or heard from me, or seen in me – put it into practice' (Phil 4:9). His shortcomings – whatever they were – lay at the back of him; he lived forward into the future through his intention to attain to Christ. He was both intent upon being like Christ (Phil 3:10–14) and confident of God's upholding grace for his intention. He could thus say to all: 'Follow me. I'm found!'

Discipleship is the found life. It's life to the full (John 10:10). It's what we were created for.

book.link

The God Chasers – Tommy Tenney, Word

Am I a disciple, or only a Christian, by current standards? Those of us who are leaders should face a second question: Is my first aim to make disciples?

Nothing less than life in the steps of Christ is adequate to the human soul or the needs of our world. Any other offer fails to do justice to the drama of human redemption, deprives the hearer of life's greatest opportunity, and abandons this present life to the evil powers of the age. The correct perspective is to see following Christ not only as the necessity it is, but as fulfilment of the highest human possibilities and as life on the highest plane.

Banquet attendance is not *required* – rather *invitations* are extended. Jesus invites us to live.

"The author of the fourth gospel puts but one question to his readers: Do we know Jesus? To know him is life. Everything else fades into twilight and darkness. For the evangelist John, what constitutes dignity in the Christian community is not apostleship or office, not titles, not the gifts of prophecy; healing, or inspired preaching, but only intimacy with Jesus. This is a status that all Christians enjoy."

– Brennan Manning

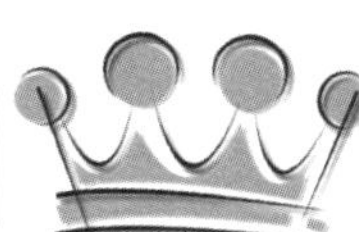

DISCIPLES IN HISTORY

The Sophists, Cynics, Stoics, Epicureans and many other philosophical schools adopted master-pupil-type discipling relationships. Socrates (470–399 BC) was a charismatic teacher to whom crowds would flock. Often pupils would pay whatever fee was demanded to sit at the feet of a teacher. Great importance was placed on learning in the Essene community. The rabbis in Jesus' time had disciples, as did the Pharisees (Matt 22:16, Mark 2:18).

"For I have come down from heaven not to do my will but to do the will of him who sent me."

– John 6:38

"You are from below; I am from above. You are of this world; I am not of this world."

– John 8:23

Freedom of Simplicity
– Richard Foster,
Triangle Books

"[9]But you are a chosen people, a royal priesthood, a holy nation, a people belonging to God, that you may declare the praises of him who called you out of darkness into his wonderful light. [10]Once you were not a people, but now you are the people of God; once you had not received mercy, but now you have received mercy. [11]Dear friends, I urge you, as aliens and strangers in the world, to abstain from sinful desires, which war against your soul. [12]Live such good lives among the pagans that, though they accuse you of doing wrong, they may see your good deeds and glorify God on the day he visits us."

– 1 Peter 2:9–12

Defining discipleship – in John's gospel

The idea of discipleship was widely accepted by the time that Jesus began his ministry. But Jesus took the idea of discipleship to a new and radical level – and we can discover the details of this as we study Jesus in John's gospel.

The disciple is a believer

So-called Doubting Thomas stands as a model of discipleship in John's gospel, in his affirmation to the risen Christ – "my Lord and my God" (John 20:28). He was able to make this statement of faith after seeing and touching the risen Jesus – but those of us who make the same pledge of allegiance (that Jesus is *our* Lord) are blessed because we have *not* seen but yet have come to believe (John 20:29). John outlines other statements of belief – like those of Martha and Peter.

A disciple of Jesus is more than a follower of his ethical and moral teaching – he or she is required to affirm a believing commitment to the divine claims of Christ.

This kind of belief and commitment should not be confused with a complete understanding, and belief in, all that Jesus requires of his followers. There is room for doubt in every disciple, alongside belief. This is powerfully expressed in the response made by the father of a boy possessed by an evil spirit who came to Jesus for healing: "I do believe; help me in my unbelief!"

The disciple is a resident alien

John uses the expression 'the world' in mostly negative terms. When it is used generally, to describe the whole of humanity, it is the object of God's love (John 3:16). Often however, it describes those who reject Jesus, who is 'not of this world' (John 6:38; 17:14–16). Thus the disciples of Jesus do not belong to this world, but as the discussion with Nicodemus shows (John 3:1–21) have been 'born again' from above, born into a new world in which Jesus belongs and from which he has come (John 17:14).

This means, in practical terms, that followers of Jesus will refuse to believe the continuously marketed notion that material gain is the substance of life and brings happiness – rather, the disciple knows that Jesus himself is the very bread of life.

It is fair to comment that such radical discipleship applied primarily

BELIEF IN JOHN

The objects of the verbs 'believe' and 'know' are virtually the same throughout the fourth gospel. The disciple is the one who believes in Jesus and through Jesus he believes in the Father who sent Jesus (e.g. John 3:16,36; 5:24; 6:29; 12:44). A variety of terms express the author's understanding of believing. It is to believe in Jesus (3:16), to believe in the Son (3:36), to believe that he is the Messiah, the Son of God (11:27; 20.31), to believe his works (10:38), and to believe in the One who sent him (12:44). But while several expressions are used, the meaning of all of them is virtually identical: they emphasize the necessity of believing in Christ in order to have eternal life. For it is in believing that a relationship with Jesus is established and maintained. The statement of purpose for writing the gospel is expressed in the same terms: "But these [signs] are written that you may believe [or "continue to believe"] that Jesus is the Christ, the Son of God, and that by believing you may have life in his name" (20:31).

In an almost identical fashion the verb 'know' involves the same themes, as in Peter's words of confession in 6:69: "We believe and know that you are the Holy One of God" (cf. 11:27). The content of knowing is Jesus, to know that he has been sent by the Father, that he is the Messiah, and – as with believing – that all this is related to eternal life: "Now this is eternal life: that they may know you, the only true God, and Jesus Christ whom you have sent" (17:3).

Discipleship is, therefore, dependent on believing in Jesus. The faith of the disciples is highlighted throughout John's gospel – even though they consistently fail to understand what is happening, often revealing a remarkable lack of insight (cf. 4:33; 13:1–11, 37; 14:1–7; 16:18). But true understanding was not possible until after the resurrection (cf. 20:9), when the Holy Spirit came. For: "The Holy Spirit ... will teach you all things and will remind you of everything I have said to you" (14:26).

– Adapted from *They Believed in Him: The Johannine Tradition* – Melvyn R. Hillmer

WORLD

World is a very significant term in John's writings. Almost without exception 'world' has negative overtones; it is the 'world' organised in rebellion against God's rule and claim. For John and for Paul the shattering thing was that the men who inhabit this beautiful and ordered universe acted in an ugly and unreasonable way when they came face to face with Christ. The world hates his followers, and he could say, "If the world hates you, keep in mind that it hated me first" (John 15:18). There is a blindness about the world. But John does not leave us with a picture of unremitting hostility between God and the world. It is true that the world is not interested in the things of God, but it is not true that God reciprocated. On the contrary God loves the world (3:16). Christ speaks to the world the things he has heard from God (8:26). The whole work of salvation that God accomplishes in Christ is directed to the world. Thus he takes away the sin of the world (1:29). He is the Saviour of the world (4:42). He gives life to the world (6:33). Of the 125 occurrences in the New Testament, 78 are in John's gospel, 24 in John's letters, and three in Revelation. This compares with eight in Matthew and three each in Mark and Luke. (Cf. 7:7; 12:31; 14:30; 15:18; 17:25.)

"I AM THE LIGHT OF THE WORLD." JOHN 8:12

This recalls the statement of the prologue: "In him was life, and that life was the light of men. The light shines in the darkness, but the darkness has not understood (overcome) it" (John 1:4–5). Jesus professed to be not only the inexhaustible source of spiritual nourishment, but also the genuine light by which truth and falsehood could be distinguished and by which direction could be established. Perhaps Jesus drew his illustration from the great candlestick, or Menorah, that was lighted during the Feast of Tabernacles and cast its light over the Court of the Women where Jesus was teaching. The Menorah was to be extinguished after the feast, but his light would remain.

"You did not choose me, but I chose you and appointed you to go and bear fruit – fruit that will last. Then the Father will give you whatever you ask in my name. This is my command: Love each other."

– John 15:16,17

Discipleship – David Watson, Hodder & Stoughton

"I believe that you are the Christ, the Son of God, who was to come into the world."

– John 11:27

"Lord, to whom shall we go? You have the words of eternal life."

– John 6:68

The Journey – Alister McGrath, Hodder & Stoughton

to those who were called into a life of full community with him. It was in the total sharing of their lives and possessions together that they were to look to God alone to meet all their needs. Other disciples who were not in such close-knit fellowship seemed to have kept at least some of their material possessions, since they helped to provide for Jesus and the twelve.

The disciple is chosen by Jesus

In rabbinical circles, a disciple would choose his own master and voluntarily join his school. But with Jesus, the initiative lay entirely with the master. Simon and Andrew, James and John, Levi, Philip and others were all personally called by Jesus to follow him. Even when the rich young ruler ran up to Jesus and asked a leading question of this good teacher, Jesus replied by spelling out the costly and total demands of discipleship, and added: "Then come, follow me" (Matt 19:21).

There may have been some who, attracted by his integrity, the quality of his teaching and by the power of his miracles, wanted to attach themselves to Jesus and to his disciples, but always it was Jesus who laid down for them the strong conditions that he required. Sometimes this proved too much for them: "This is more than we can stomach! Why listen to such words?" (John 6:60 NEB). And they left him, leaving only the twelve whom he had chosen and called to himself after a whole night spent in prayer. These were the ones in particular that God had given him (John 17:9). Yet although there is a uniqueness about the twelve apostles, this fact of God's initiative and Christ's calling lies behind all those who are his disciples.

Three points of interest arise from that particular statement.

- A disciple is a chosen servant, not an enthusiastic volunteer
- A disciple is chosen irrespective of qualifications
- A disciple is chosen for community, not isolated spirituality

The disciple journeys with Jesus

Eduard Schweizer, writing about the relationship between Jesus and his disciples:

"... the disciples walk with him, eat and drink with him, listen to what he says and see what he does, are invited with him into houses and hovels, or are turned away with him. They are not called to great achievements, religious or otherwise. They are invited as companions to share in what takes place around Jesus. They are

OUR ATTITUDE TO BEING PERSONALLY CHOSEN BY JESUS

If we have been personally chosen by Jesus, this should alter our whole attitude towards him and motivate us for the work he has given us. If someone is chosen to represent his country for the Olympics, his whole attitude and approach to his event will be quite different from someone who has himself chosen to go as a spectator. With the first, there will be a total and sacrificial dedication to the task, partly because of the privilege of having been chosen. There will be a strong sense of responsibility which even the most enthusiastic tourist will not have. The Church today suffers from large numbers who feel that *they* have made a decision for Christ, or from those who think that *they* have chosen to join a certain church. Such man-centred notions spell spiritual death, or at least barren sterility. It is only when we begin to see ourselves as chosen, called and commissioned by Christ that we shall have any real sense of our responsibility "to offer your bodies as living sacrifices, holy and pleasing to God" (Rom 12:1).

Certainly the apostles could not get away from this awareness of divine constraint.

"Unlike so many, we do not peddle the word of God for profit. On the contrary, in Christ we speak before God with sincerity, like men sent from God" (2 Cor 2:17).

"Therefore, since through God's mercy we have this ministry, we do not lose heart" (2 Cor 4:1).

"Paul, a servant of Christ Jesus, called to be an apostle and set apart for the gospel of God – ... [7]To all in Rome who are loved by God and called to be saints:" (Rom 1:1,7).

"For we know, brothers loved by God, that he has chosen you," (1 Thess 1:4).

"You are not your own; you were bought at a price. Therefore honour God with your body" (1 Cor 6:19,20).

Such examples could be multiplied again and again. It was this strong sense of God's calling, of Christ's initiative, of the Spirit's sovereign work, that enabled them to be bold in their witness, to hold fast in their suffering, and to lead lives 'worthy of the calling' they had received (Eph 4:1). – *David Watson*

SECTION 2

JESUS THE DISCIPLER

Peter turned and saw that the disciple whom Jesus loved was following them. (This was the one who had leaned back against Jesus at the supper and had said, "Lord, who is going to betray you?") [21]When Peter saw him, he asked, "Lord, what about him?"
[22]Jesus answered, "If I want him to remain alive until I return, what is that to you? You must follow me."
[23]Because of this, the rumour spread among the brothers that this disciple would not die. But Jesus did not say that he would not die; he only said, "If I want him to remain alive until I return, what is that to you?"

– John 21:20–23

'... he poured water into a basin and began to wash his disciples' feet, drying them with the towel that was wrapped around him.'

– John 13:5

book.link

Patterns of Discipleship in the New Testament – Richard N. Longenecker, Eerdmans

therefore called not to attach much importance to themselves and what they accomplish or fail to accomplish, but to attach great importance to what takes place through Jesus and with him."

The call *by* Jesus was also a call *to* Jesus. The Jewish rabbi and the Greek philosopher expected disciples to commit themselves to a specific teaching or to a definite cause.

In the case of Judaism, it was the Law, the Torah, that was at the centre of the relationship between a rabbi and disciple. The authority rested in the Law, not the teacher. But Jesus went far beyond what any Jewish rabbi could have said, in calling his disciples to lose their lives for *his* sake (Matt 10:39). The call of Jesus was wholly personal: his disciples were to follow him, to be with him, and to commit themselves wholeheartedly to him.

John's gospel specifically underlines this **relational** element in discipleship in the teaching of:

- The Good Shepherd (John 10)
- The Vine and the Branches (John 15)
- The Restoration of Peter (John 21)
- The example of the 'disciple whom Jesus loved' (John 21:20)
- Martha and Mary (John 11)
- Not 'inviting Jesus into my heart' but travelling, journeying with him.
- The life of discipleship is not a one-off choice, but rather a daily decision to follow Jesus and be with him. Salvation is a life lived, a journey along the way, not a crisis event.

Well-known broadcaster Simon Mayo has written an article that expresses his desire to lose the tag Christian. He suggests, tongue in cheek, that we should be called Mounties (as in Sermon on the Mount-*ies*).

The disciple is a servant

The disciples of the rabbis were only their *students* – not their *servants*. This was profoundly radical teaching from Jesus. Although the disciples were called by Jesus first and foremost to be with him, they were also commissioned to go and preach the kingdom of heaven and "heal the sick, raise the dead" (Matt 10:8). Jesus had come to lay down his life for the sake of others, and his disciples were called by him to do exactly the same. Yet they did not always understand this.

The servant heart is expressed in a humility and willingness to submit to each other 'out of reverence for Christ' (Eph 5:21).

CALLED TO A PERSON

The personal allegiance of the disciples to Jesus is confirmed by their conduct in the days between the crucifixion and the resurrection. The reason for the deep depression which marks these days is to be found in the fate which has befallen the person of Jesus. No matter what view we take of the story of the walk to Emmaus, the fact that "he" is the theme of their conversation on the way (Luke 24:19ff) corresponds in every sense to the relation of the disciples to Jesus before his arrest and execution. On the other hand, it is nowhere stated or even hinted that after the death of Jesus his teaching was a source of strength to his followers, or that they had the impression of having a valuable legacy in the word of Jesus. This is a point of considerable importance for a true understanding of the *mathetes* of Jesus.

After the horrifying events of the crucifixion it took some time for Jesus to restore the faith and commitment of his disciples. But he did this by leading them gently back into a renewed relationship with him. After Peter's threefold denial comes the threefold question by Jesus, "Simon, son of John, do you love me?" Repeatedly, in his resurrection appearances, he came to his disciples, individually and corporately, to reassure them of his living presence, and of his love and forgiveness. They were to become witnesses to him – not rabbis of his teaching. They were to tell everyone about him, and, in the sharing of their lives together, to manifest his life by being the body of Christ on earth.

When Buddha was dying, his disciples asked how they could best remember him. He told them not to bother. It was his teaching, not his person, that counted. With Jesus it is altogether different. Everything centres round him. Discipleship means knowing him, loving him, believing in him, being committed to him. – *Kittel's Theological Dictionary of the New Testament* (Vol.4)

BREAD OF LIFE

The assertion "I am the bread of life" (John 6:48) is the first in a series of such declarations that are peculiar to John's gospel (8:12; 10:7,11; 11:25; 14:6; 15:1). Each represents a particular relationship of Jesus to the spiritual needs of men, their light in darkness, entrance into security and fellowship, their guide and protector in life, their hope in death, their certainty in perplexity, and their source of vitality for productiveness. He desired that men should receive him, not simply for what he might give them, but for what he might be to them. The use of the definite article 'the' in 'the life' is definitive and restrictive. Jesus was talking about 'the' bread that gives eternal life; but this was beyond their comprehension, just as the miracles Jesus had performed in their sight did not lead them to believe in him. Jesus links the statement to life itself. When the Jews ate the heavenly bread (*manna*) in the wilderness, their physical needs were met. However, they still died (v.49). But Jesus said that he was "the bread that comes down from heaven, which a man may eat and not die" (v.50).

JESUS THE DISCIPLER

"I tell you the truth, the Son can do nothing by himself; he can do only what he sees his Father doing, because whatever the Father does the Son also does."

– John 5:19

"We are not called to make waves. We are called to ride the waves that God makes."

– anon

"The great tragedy of modern evangelism is in calling many to belief but few to obedience."

– Jim Wallis

"For it has been granted to you on behalf of Christ not only to believe on him, but also to suffer for him."

– Phil 1:29

"This is not an age in which to be a soft Christian."

– Francis Schaeffer

"Joy and woe are woven fine."

– William Blake

Jesus demonstrated this spirit of service in a way they never forgot, when he wrapped a towel around his waist and washed their feet (John 13:5).

? **Do you have a servant's heart, ready to receive loving confrontation from friends around you? Are you a teachable person – or do people feel the need to 'walk on eggshells' when you come by?**

The disciple watches Jesus at work

Watching Jesus at work

The disciple is not called to make it happen but rather to be a witness of what Jesus is doing and in our case to allow him to work his works through us – hence the blunt statement that without him we can do nothing.

Learning from the Jesus approach

Jesus frequently manoeuvres his disciples into learning situations, provoking them to take action, wanting them to learn the lessons of life. He prompts them to feed the crowds, puzzles them with his teaching and encourages them to ask him questions. They learn mostly through their mistakes.

The discipling relationship never ends

The disciples of a Jewish rabbi would submit themselves as slaves to their master until such time when they could leave their schooling and become masters or rabbis themselves. But Jesus calls his disciples to unconditional obedience for the whole of their lives. We shall never graduate this side of heaven. We shall never get beyond a life of obedience. To obey God's will is to find the fulfilment of our lives.

So complete is the commitment to follow Jesus that John's gospel shows us Jesus telling his disciples that they cannot immediately follow him into death (John 13:36).

To be a disciple of Jesus means to follow him, to go the way that he goes, to accept his plan and will for our lives. There is no true faith without obedience, and there is no discipleship either.

BIND US TO JESUS

I have a longing past conveying ... to use whatever gifts of persuasion I may have to induce others to see that they must at all costs hold on to the reality of Christ; to lash themselves to the mast when storms blow up and the seas are rough. For indeed without a doubt, storms and rough seas lie ahead. We need urgently in the Church today true disciples who will bind themselves to Jesus Christ in unswerving obedience and loyalty. – *Malcolm Muggeridge*

A TEACHABLE HEART

One evening, I stopped by the church just to encourage those who were rehearsing there for the spring musical. I didn't intend to stay long so I parked my car next to the entrance. After a few minutes I ran back to my car and drove home.

The next morning I found a note in my office mail box. It read: "A small thing, but Tuesday night when you came to rehearsal you parked in the 'No Parking' area. A reaction from one of my crew (who did not recognise you after you got out of your car) was, 'There's another jerk in the "No Parking" area!' We try hard not to allow people – even workers – to park anywhere other than the parking lot. I would appreciate your cooperation too." It was signed by a member of our maintenance staff.

This man's stock went up in my book because he had the courage to write to me about what could have been a slippage in my character. And he was right on the mark. As I drove up that night I had thought, 'I shouldn't park here, but after all, I am the pastor.' That translates, 'I am an exception to the rules.' But that employee wouldn't allow me to sneak down the road labelled 'I am an exception.' I am not the exception to church rules or any of God's rules. As a leader I am not an exception: I'm to be the example. According to Scripture, I am to live in such a way that I can say: "Follow me. Park where I park. Live as I live." – *Bill Hybels, the dynamic young leader of the 20,000-strong Willow Creek Community Church in the USA*

SUFFERING

Peter and John were imprisoned and later beaten for their boldness; Stephen was stoned to death, and James killed with the sword. Before long a great persecution arose against the Church in Jerusalem, and they were all scattered.

Paul later wrote about being beaten five times with the 39 lashes of the Jewish whip, three times with rods, and once stoned. According to various Christian traditions, most if not all the apostles suffered eventual martyrdom of one form or another. During those early years of the Church waves of bitter and appalling persecution came from a succession of Roman emperors: Nero, Domitian, Trajan, Pliny, Marcus Aurelius, Decius and Diocletian. In various degrees of ferocity this continued up to AD 305, and of course has continued throughout the entire history of the Christian Church. It is sobering to remember that in recent years countless thousands of Christians have been imprisoned and tortured for their faith, and are still being so today in various parts of the world. It is estimated that there have been more martyrdoms for Christ this century than during the rest of the Church's history.

Suffering is inescapably woven into the fabric of discipleship. But we shall often discover that it is in the midst of suffering that God is working most profoundly in our lives.

One Christian who spent over ten years in a Communist prison in Czechoslovakia for his faith in Christ said that his torturers broke his bones but not his spirit. He referred to those years as the richest years of his life. "We must pray, not that persecution will not come, but that we may be worthy of it, open to the blessings God offers through it."

SECTION 2
JESUS THE DISCIPLER

BIBLE PASSAGE

John 5:16–30

16So, because Jesus was doing these things on the Sabbath, the
Jews persecuted him. 17Jesus said to them, "My Father is always
at his work to this very day, and I, too, am working." 18For this
reason the Jews tried all the harder to kill him; not only was he
breaking the Sabbath, but he was even calling God his own
Father, making himself equal with God.

19Jesus gave them this answer: "I tell you the truth, the Son can
do nothing by himself; he can do only what he sees his Father
doing, because whatever the Father does the Son also does. 20For
the Father loves the Son and shows him all he does. Yes, to your
amazement he will show him even greater things than these.
21For just as the Father raises the dead and gives them life, even
so the Son gives life to whom he is pleased to give it. 22Moreover,
the Father judges no one, but has entrusted all judgment to the
Son, 23that all may honour the Son just as they honour the Father.
He who does not honour the Son does not honour the Father,
who sent him.

24"I tell you the truth, whoever hears my word and believes him
who sent me has eternal life and will not be condemned; he has
crossed over from death to life. 25I tell you the truth, a time is
coming and has now come when the dead will hear the voice of
the Son of God and those who hear will live. 26For as the Father
has life in himself, so he has granted the Son to have life in
himself. 27And he has given him authority to judge because he is
the Son of Man.

28"Do not be amazed at this, for a time is coming when all who
are in their graves will hear his voice 29and come out – those who
have done good will rise to live, and those who have done evil
will rise to be condemned. 30By myself I can do nothing; I judge
only as I hear, and my judgment is just, for I seek not to please
myself but him who sent me.

Comment

The Radical Jesus –

v17	His work
v18	And relationship
	with the Father offends the religious and the traditionalists.

The Reliant Jesus –

v19	He works in total cooperation and teamwork with the Father
	The triune God is the greatest model of teamwork.

The Resurrected Jesus –

v24	who has in him eternal life and pardon
v25,29	and who speaks even to death and it obeys

Jesus' modus operandi –

v30	'Not to please myself, but him'

NOTES

SECTION 2
JESUS THE DISCIPLER

The discipling community

Church: Information centre, where the word is faithfully preached? Worship centre, where sacrament and song are shared? Or both of these and more – a community of disciples, growing together in Jesus?

If our churches are to become discipling churches, then we need to clear up three potential misunderstandings.

- **Misunderstanding 1 – discipleship is for new Christians only**. Discipleship is not just about the nurture of new Christians. It's a lifelong process.
- **Misunderstanding 2 – discipleship is about 'heavy shepherding'**. The word 'discipleship' fell into disrepute in the 1970s, with some groups practising an unhealthy level of control and supervision of their members, and all done in the name of discipleship. This was rooted in an unbiblical understanding of the nature of authority, and a commitment to pyramid type structures of church leadership that were unhelpful and contrary to the spirit of Scripture.
- **Misunderstanding 3 – disciples just need to be fed: all it requires is more preaching**. We have largely developed a model in the Church that is pulpit-centred. The suggestion is that if we simply gather faithfully to hear the scriptures preached, then this will be sufficient to produce disciples. **This is not true, according to the Jesus model.**

In Jesus, we find the most effective, dynamic and Holy Spirit-anointed communicator in the history of civilisation – but he didn't rely solely on preaching and teaching in order to make disciples. He shared his life with his followers, modelling truth, steering them into problems that they were called to solve, provoking their questions, rebuking them when necessary. Although there were many public discourses, the main work of discipling was done in a more relational, interactive environment when informal question and answer sessions flowed naturally.

If we are to make disciples, preaching and teaching, though vital, are not enough. Courses for new Christians can be helpful, but ultimately will not generally provide for the parenting needs of new believers.

We must not confuse our commitment to Scripture with a commitment to a style of preaching and proclaiming the word of God.

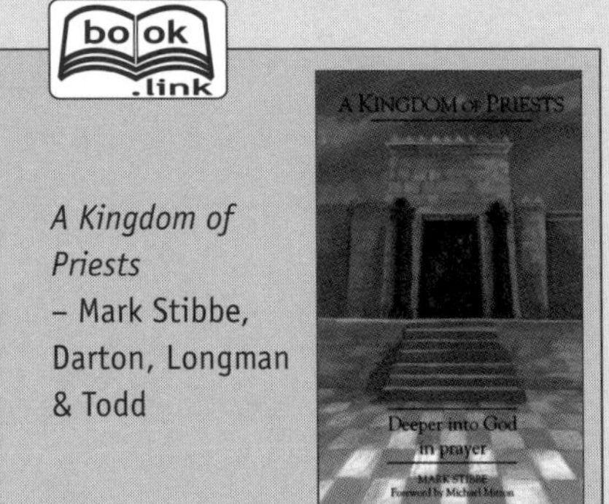

A Kingdom of Priests – Mark Stibbe, Darton, Longman & Todd

"The task of the Church is not to make men and women happy – it is to make them holy."

– Chuck Colson

MODERN MARTYR

This note was found in the office of a young pastor in Zimbabwe after his martyrdom for his faith in Jesus Christ.

I'm part of the fellowship of the unashamed. I have the Holy Spirit power. The die has been cast. I have stepped over the line. The decision has been made—I'm a disciple of his. I won't look back, let up, slow down, back away, or be still. My past is redeemed, my present makes sense, my future is secure. I'm finished and done with low living, sight walking, smooth knees, colourless dreams, tamed visions, worldly talking, cheap giving, and dwarfed goals.

I no longer need preeminence, prosperity, position, promotions, plaudits, or popularity. I don't have to be right, first, tops, recognized, praised, regarded, or rewarded. I now live by faith, lean in his presence, walk by patience, am uplifted by prayer, and I labour with power.

My life is set, my gait is fast, my goal is heaven, my road is narrow, my way rough, my companions are few, my guide reliable, my mission clear. I cannot be bought, compromised, detoured, lured away, turned back, deluded, or delayed. I will not flinch in the face of sacrifice, hesitate in the presence of the enemy, pander at the pool of popularity, or meander in the maze of mediocrity.

I won't give up, shut up, let up, until I have stayed up, stored up, prayed up, paid up, preached up for the cause of Christ. I am a disciple of Jesus. I must go till he comes, give till I drop, preach till all know, and work till he stops me. And when he comes for his own, he will have no problem recognizing me. My banner will be clear!

GET REAL

RISK – Paul took the risk of writing to the contentious Corinthians to spell out the sense of despair that he had been feeling (2 Cor 1:9): "Indeed, in our hearts we felt the sentence of death. But this happened that we might not rely on ourselves but on God, who raises the dead."

REVIVAL – A commitment to reality and openness is a sign of genuine revival (Acts 19:18): "Many of those who believed now came and openly confessed their evil deeds."

REAL FELLOWSHIP – Scripture affirms that light and accountability are vital for true fellowship (1 John 1:7): "But if we walk in the light, as he is in the light, we have fellowship with one another, and the blood of Jesus, his Son, purifies us from all sin."

What is a discipling church like?

A church of reality and vulnerability rather than image and performance.

Jesus is revealed in John's gospel as the one who was unafraid to weep (John 11:35), who felt weary and who asked for refreshment (John 4:7), and who shared with his disciples a hatred of the world (John 15:18,19).

He is real about his emotions and needs – and if we are to build communities in his name, we must look for the same level of authenticity.

"Pretending is the common cold of evangelicalism."

– Gordon McDonald

A church that is a pastoring community rather than a church with a pastor.

If we take the Jesus model seriously, and he tried to disciple only twelve at one time, why do we try to designate the pastoral care of hundreds of people to one person?

This is not to devalue leadership – on the contrary, it is to value and release leaders to do that which God has really called them to do, to equip the saints (us) for the work of the ministry (Eph 4:11–12), rather than trying to do all the ministry themselves.

And what about students away from their churches at university? At this critical and formative time in their lives, small group interaction and involvement can be a vital resource for discipleship.

**"13Is any one of you in trouble?
He should pray. Is anyone happy?
Let him sing songs of praise. 14Is
any one of you sick? He should
call the elders of the church to
pray over him and anoint him with
oil in the name of the Lord. 15And
the prayer offered in faith will
make the sick person well; the
Lord will raise him up. If he has
sinned, he will be forgiven.
16Therefore confess your sins to
each other and pray for each other
so that you may be healed."**

– James 5:13–16

A church that equips people for real life with relevant teaching, both in terms of content and presentation.

Why is it that most Christians spend most of their lives in the workplace, yet there are so few sermons about the workplace in local churches?

Jesus drew most of his illustrations from everyday life, from the lives of those around him, from keen and accurate observation. More than anything else he told stories to illustrate his point and to make truth relevant and applicable.

He used short stories (parables), questions, humour and riddles. He often used questions to answer questions and frequently his questions went right to the heart of the matter.

He often entered into dialogue rather than give dictation.

FREEDOM TO STRUGGLE

Weakness, vulnerability and powerlessness are central to Christian belief – and to the extent that Christians fail to model that in both lifestyle and evangelistic communication, they are betraying the very gospel they claim to represent.

We must build churches where people experience freedom to struggle and doubt – communities where doubts can be expressed without fear of censure, where people are encouraged to explore their uncertainties, rather than toeing a party line.

We must build churches where unbelief and unquestioned beliefs are recognized as the enemies of faith, but doubt is valued as a spur to growth. Thomas, famous for his doubts, was not rejected by his apostolic colleagues, but was present with them the next time Jesus appeared to his disciples, and doubt gave way to faith and worship (John 20:24–28). **Dishonesty,** rather than honest argument, must be recognized as a threat to unity.

We must build churches where people experience opportunities to explore different views, learn to listen to other perspectives and are not threatened if they cannot identify 'the answer' to every question. This is not because these churches believe nothing, but because they are not afraid to subject their beliefs to scrutiny. Their core convictions are the basis for this free and generous spirit.

SHAKEN AND RECONCILED

E. Stanley Jones, the great evangelist, once wrote of a time early in his Christian experience. "For months after my conversion, I was running under cloudless skies. And then suddenly I tripped, almost fell, pulled back this side of the sin, but was shaken and humiliated that I could come that close to sin. I thought I was emancipated and found I wasn't."

Then he goes on to write of the effort of special friends who played the intercessory position:

"I went to the class meeting – I'm grateful that I didn't stay away – I went, but my (spiritual) music had gone. I had hung my harp on a weeping willow tree. As the others spoke of their joys and victories of the week, I sat there with the tears rolling down my cheeks. I was heartbroken. After the others had spoken, John Zink, the class leader, said: "Now, Stanley, tell us what is the matter." I told them I couldn't but would they please pray for me? Like one man they fell to their knees, and they lifted me back to the bosom of God by faith and love. When we got up from our knees, I was reconciled. The universe opened its arms and took me in again. The estrangement was gone. I took my heart from the willow tree and began to sing again."
– *E. Stanley Jones, A Song of Ascents*

Quoted in *Restoring your Spiritual Passion,* by Gordon MacDonald

STEPS TOWARD A PASTORING COMMUNITY

This may be achieved by

- Developing a pastoral team.
- Fostering a general atmosphere of mutual care.
- Developing teams of specialist ministries, e.g. hospital visitations, etc.
- Commitment to see leadership as a team function rather than the function of just one 'specialist' person.
- Refusal to adopt the typical divides between clergy and laity.

SECTION 2
JESUS THE DISCIPLER

"What people learn in the first few months of their Christian life is what they are likely to be in the rest of their Christian life, short of an explosion to blow them up! Therefore, what they hear and the environment they meet within the church when they first arrive is vitally important."

– Roger Forster

A church that is committed to the nurture and care of new Christians

New Christians are vulnerable – the Parable of the Sower (Matt 13:3–9) makes that clear.

In nurturing new Christians, we should seek to help them

- to walk with Jesus in their new lifestyle
- to become rooted in the family of believers
- in their understanding of Scripture as truth
- realise the privilege of discipleship in service, mission, etc.

We should not assume that they

- know what to do during our public meetings
- know anything about Christianity
- understand our language or jargon
- run a filofax-driven life, as is the case in evangelical culture
- want to pray out loud or read Scripture out loud
- will be stable or consistent
- will understand theological ideas – example and modelling are better.

We must

- prioritise important issues – rather than dumping a Bible on them and hoping they'll sort it out
- be available
- be gentle
- don't take authority – just explain, point out and persuade
- encourage
- pray for them.

My First Trousers – Mike Pilavachi, Hodder & Stoughton

A church that practises discipleship and discipline

Discipleship and discipline. Those two words look rather similar, don't they? Jesus engaged in a number of disciplines that will help us, if we engage in them too. Spiritual disciplines – things like prayer, fasting, solitude and celebration – are activities that can help us to grow more like Jesus.

Dallas Willard describes them thus: "A discipline of the spiritual life is, when the dust of history is blown away, nothing but an activity undertaken to bring us into more effective cooperation with Christ and his kingdom. When we understand that grace (*charis*) is gift (*charisma*), we then see that to grow in grace is to grow in what is

Body & Cell – Howard Astin, Monarch

RADICAL STRUCTURES

Some churches have seen small groups or cell groups as a way to move the church further towards being an evangelistic and discipleship based community.

There is a further plus.link about Urban Expression's radical approach on Page 89.

A CHURCH IN TRANSITION

Holy Trinity Church, Hazlemere, Buckinghamshire

Holy Trinity is a local Anglican church that has benefited from continuity of leadership – with just two vicars presiding over the last thirty years, Rev Clive Collier being the latest leader. The church had in excess of 500 members, about half of which were in long-standing small groups, and it was generally lively and outward-looking. The church then split down into four congregations – meeting in local schools as well as the main church building. With this downsizing came new small groups, with new leaders – each group containing about 6 or 7 members. However, the leadership had not heard of 'cell church'.

In the early part of 1995, Clive Collier began to hear from a friend in Bradford that the model Holy Trinity was adopting was in fact moving towards cell church. It was decided that they would shut down the existing small groups which they did in March 1995. In April of that year around 40 leaders went away to seek God together, and then in May some of the leaders attended the Cell Conference. Following this, a handbook was issued to each church member to explain the coming changes, and everyone was encouraged to transfer to one of the 30 new cells that had been formed. The church is parish-based and the majority of the cells are geographically defined – some encompassing a single street. The initial result was that around 85–90 per cent of those in old small groups transferred.

Clive Collier and his leadership are realistic about the difficulties of transition. Derek Hopwood, who is responsible for much of the 'nuts and bolts' of the cells recognises that whilst the majority of the groups have started well, not all of them will necessarily work in the long run. "We didn't have a layer of experienced leaders to draw upon and suddenly we needed 30 cells leaders!" The church has run monthly training sessions fort the leaders, plus full day events and meetings to impart vision. "We recognised that our number one issue is the support of the groups leaders," Derek says.

Initially all of the "Zone" supervision has been carried out by members of the Eldership of the church, but this is evolving to a more congregationally based system. Feedback is aided by the weekly sheet of notes for the cell meetings – produced by Clive Collier – which also includes categories for assessing the meetings.

Holy Trinity is running Alpha groups alongside their cell structure and this has been successful. Two groups multiplied quickly, due to new believers coming through Alpha.

The leadership are very positive about the benefits the new cell emphasis has brought. Every member is being encouraged in ministry and the new leaders are doing well.

given to us by God. The disciplines are then, in the clearest sense, a means to that grace and also to those gifts. Spiritual disciplines, 'exercises unto godliness', are only activities undertaken to make us capable of receiving more of his life and power without harm to ourselves or others." (*The Spirit of the Disciplines)*

But many people, over the years, have misunderstood and misused them.

Clearing the decks for discipline

Discipline is a word against which we can tend to react – it has negative connotations for many people because:

- spiritual discipline is apparently attacked by Hebrew prophets – and Jesus himself. Some would try to argue that Isaiah and the Lord himself spoke against practices like fasting and rituals of worship, for example in Isaiah 58 and Matthew 23. In reality, neither was speaking out against them, but rather against their abuse. So fasting in an attempt to manipulate God, or impress others, is wrong. Jesus is not writing off the disciplines – rather he is seeking to protect their integrity.

- a historical hangover lingers on – a sense that discipline has to do with self-mutilation and hatred of the body. Inevitably there have always been those who take a principle of self-denial and attempt to live it to excess. No one would question the motives of those who practised extreme self-denial (although some historians would suggest that there was a competitive spirit sometimes between some of the extreme ascetics of the past), but they were definitely in need of wisdom.

Martin Luther despised the spiritual exercises that had driven him prior to his discovery of justification by faith. He nearly died because of his excessive practice of fasting. We should remember that Luther was endeavouring to find redemption and grace by practising the disciplines in a legalistic manner. Again, the problem was with the misuse of the disciplines.

Let's recognise that spiritual discipline has nothing to do with self-inflicted pain, 'masochism' or hatred of the body. It does not have any merit in and of itself – so we do not 'worship worship' or prayer. Spiritual discipline has nothing to do with obtaining grace – we discipline ourselves because we have received grace.

"Celibacy, fasting, penance, mortification, self-denial, humility, silence, solitude, and the whole train of monkish virtues: – for what reason are they everywhere rejected by men of sense, but because they serve to no manner of purpose; neither advance a man's fortune in the world, nor render him a more valuable member of society; neither qualify him for the entertainment of company, nor increase his power of self-enjoyment? We observe, on the contrary, that they cross all these desirable ends; stupefy the understanding and harden the heart, obscure the fancy and sour the temper ... A gloomy, hair-brained enthusiast, after death, may have a place in the calendar; but will scarcely ever be admitted, when alive, into intimacy and society, except by those who are as delirious and dismal as himself..."

– *David Hume,* 18th-century writer and thinker

"The disciplines place us before God; they do not give us brownie points with God."

– *Richard Foster*

QUIET TIMES

A few years ago, some Christian speakers were heard to question the practice of having a 'quiet time' (a regular period of daily prayer). They suggested that engaging in such a habit meant that the person was seeking to win God's approval by, for example, getting up to pray in the early hours of the day.

The teaching contained a grain of truth, because the length and timing of our prayers cannot change the amount of love God has for us. We pray because of the grace of God, and not to win or earn the grace of God.

There was an unhelpful result of this teaching, however, in that some dismissed the discipline of prayer fearing legalism. In fact it is the misuse of the discipline that causes it to become a religious trap.

LUTHER AND THE DISCIPLINES

Luther believed that he would ultimately have killed himself if he had continued his slavish commitment to prayers, vigils, reading, fasting, and other exercises of discipline.

He fasted, sometimes three days on end without a crumb. The seasons of fasting were more consoling to him than those of feasting. Lent was more comforting than Easter. He laid upon himself vigils and prayers in excess of those stipulated by the rule. He cast off the blankets permitted him and well nigh froze himself to death. At times he was proud of his sanctity and would say 'I have done nothing wrong today'. Then misgivings would arise. 'Have you fasted enough? Are you poor enough'? He would then strip himself of all save that which decency required. He believed in later life that his austerities had done permanent damage to his digestion.'
– Roland Bainton, Here I Stand

WILD MEN AND WOMEN OF THE DESERT

Macarius of Alexandria ate no cooked food for seven years. Deliberately exposing his naked body to poisonous flies, he slept in a marsh for six months.

Some ascetics could boast that they had not laid down to sleep for fifty years. Others kept a record of how many years it had been since they had even set eyes upon a woman.

Simeon Stylites (AD 309–459) built a column six feet high in the Syrian desert. He became dissatisfied with its size and found one sixty feet high, and three feet across, where he sat for thirty years, exposed to rain and sun and cold. A ladder enabled disciples to take him food and remove his waste. He bound himself to the pillar by a rope, the rope became embedded in his flesh, which putrefied around it, and stank, and teemed with worms. Simeon picked up the worms which fell from his sores and replaced them there saying to them, 'Eat what God has given you'.

The Irish saint Finnchua spent seven years suspended by his armpits in iron shackles. He and St. Ite deliberately allowed their bodies to be eaten by beetles. St. Ciaran mixed his bread with sand, and St. Kevin refused to sit down for seven years. Wearing hair shirts, self-flagellation and involuntary dancing were all practised by the rival orders of St. Francis and St. Dominic. – *Will Durant, The Age of Faith*

Wild woman Clarissa refused to wash at all following her conversion – no part of her body was to touch water, save her fingertips. Her 'abstinence' had a startling effect – it was said that 'she dropped vermin while she walked'.

SECTION 2

JESUS THE DISCIPLER

As we embrace a life of spiritual discipline, we make deliberate choices to so order our lives in such a way that we can consciously receive the grace of God, which will ultimately lead to our being transformed into being like Christ.

book.link

Celebration of Discipline – Richard Foster, Hodder & Stoughton

Richard Foster in his classic book *Celebration of Discipline* provides a helpful warning list of pitfalls:

- **Turning the disciplines into law.** 'There is nothing like legalism to choke the heart and soul out of walking with God. The rigid person is not the disciplined person. Rigidity is the most certain sign that the disciplines have gone to seed. The disciplined person can do what needs to be done when it needs to be done.'

- **Failure to understand the social implications of the disciplines.** 'These are not a set of pious exercises for the devout, but a trumpet call to obedient living in a sin-racked world. They call us to wage peace in a world obsessed with war, to plead for justice in a world plagued with inequity, to stand with the poor and disinherited in a world that has forgotten its neighbour.'

- **Viewing the disciplines as virtuous in themselves.** 'In and of themselves the disciplines have no virtue, possess no righteousness, contain no rectitude. It was this important truth that the Pharisees failed to see. The disciplines place us before God; they do not give us brownie points with God.'

- **To centre on the disciplines rather than on Christ.** 'The disciplines are for the purpose of realising a greater good. And that greater good is Christ himself, who must always remain the focus of our attention and the end of our quest.'

- **The tendency to isolate and elevate one discipline to the exclusion or neglect of the others.** 'The disciplines are like the fruit of the Spirit – they comprise a single reality. Sometimes we become intrigued with fasting, for example, and we begin to think of that single discipline as comprising the whole picture. What is only one tree we see as the whole forest. This danger must be avoided at all costs. The disciplines of the spiritual life are an organic unity, a single path.'

- **To think that any prescribed list of disciplines somehow exhausts the means of God's grace.** 'I have no exhaustive list of the Christian disciplines and as far as I know none exists, for who can confine the Spirit of God?'

"For those God foreknew he also predestined to be conformed to the likeness of his Son, that he might be the firstborn among many brothers."

– Romans 8:29

NO PAIN, NO GAIN?

For nearly seven hundred years 'the discipline' was in fact a whip used to flagellate oneself during times of penance and prayer. Various models were available – thorn branches braided together, iron chains, or leather straps tipped with metal or bone. From the 13th through to the 19th century *the discipline* was a whip made of strands of rope knotted at the ends.

DEFINING DISCIPLINE

Though we may not be aware of it, we experience 'disciplines' every day. In these daily or 'natural' disciplines we perform acts that result in a direct command of further abilities that we would not otherwise have. If I repeat the telephone number aloud after looking it up, I can remember it until I get it dialled. Otherwise, I probably couldn't. If I train rigorously I can bench press 300 pounds; otherwise not. Such ordinary activities are actually disciplines that aid our physical or 'natural' life.

The same thing happens with disciplines for our spiritual life. When through spiritual disciplines I become able heartily to bless those who curse me, pray without ceasing, to be at peace when not given credit for good deeds I've done, or to master the evil that comes my way, it is because my disciplinary activities have inwardly prepared me for more and more interaction with the powers of the living God and his kingdom. Such is the potential we tap into when we use the disciplines. – *Dallas Willard, The Spirit of the Disciplines*

"Have nothing to do with godless myths and old wives' tales; rather, train yourself to be godly. [8]For physical training is of some value, but godliness has value for all things, holding promise for both the present life and the life to come."

– 1 Tim 4:7–8

An Affair of the Heart
– Robert Warren, HB

"Lord, teach us to pray, just as John taught his disciples."

– Luke 11:1b

Daily Devotions Made Easy
– Mark Water, OM

Get down to the gym

Jesus deliberately and consciously chose to prioritise the work that his Father had given him to do – his 'food and drink' was to obey the Father (John 4:34). The result of that choice was a daily, disciplined existence that would enable him to complete the work that he was sent to do.

Choices are important – but they must be followed through with discipline, as anybody who has ever made a New Year's resolution will surely confirm.

Paul instructs his disciple and friend Timothy to train himself for godliness (1 Tim 4:7–8).

The Greek word for 'train' is *gumnaze* – the root for our word gymnasium. Paul, the man who loved to use sporting analogies in his writings, is exhorting Timothy and all would-be disciples that serious disciplined decisions have to be taken in order to walk in a godly life. To quote the old cliche: 'If we fail to plan, then we plan to fail.'

How often are well-intentioned 'decisions' made at large events like Spring Harvest, but remain just that – good intentions that never grow into reality. How many people have ever purchased a subscription to a gym or sports club – but failed to actually make use of the facilities?

The disciplines that Jesus followed

There is second hand gym equipment for sale – previously used by Jesus. If it helped him, it's worth us looking at the practices that he embraced.

Communion with Father – prayer

As a Jew, Jesus would have recited the *Shema*, a statement of faith, twice each day:

'Hear O Israel, the Lord our God is one Lord' (Deut 6:4)

And also observed the three hours of prayer, in the morning, afternoon and at sundown. The hours of prayer would conclude with the chanting of the *Tephilla*, a number of benedictions.

- Such was the quality of Jesus' own prayer life that those close to him asked him for prayer lessons (Luke 11:1)
- He found prayer more appealing than crowds (Luke 5:15–16), often rising early in the morning to pray (Mark 1:35): it was in

I'LL TELL YOU WHAT I WANT, WHAT I REALLY REALLY WANT...

There are many people I know who possess a vision of personal evolution yet seem to lack the will for it. They want, and believe it is possible, to skip over the discipline, to find an easy short cut to sainthood. Often they attempt to attain it by simply imitating the superficialities of saints, retiring to the desert or taking up carpentry. Some even believe that by such imitation they have really become saints and prophets, and are unable to acknowledge that they are still children and face the painful fact that they must start at the beginning and go through the middle... . – *M. Scott Peck, psychiatrist, The Road Less Travelled*

prayer that Jesus learned the Father's will

- He gave himself to more intense seasons of prayer at certain times in his ministry – for example at decisive times of change. His baptism, which signalled the beginning of his public ministry, was followed by an extended period of prayer
- He spent whole nights in prayer. Before appointment of the twelve (Luke 6:12) and during the season of temple teaching (Luke 21:37–38) Jesus lost sleep for prayer. He prayed before he raised Lazarus (John 11:41–42).

"Prayer – secret, fervent, believing prayer – lies at the root of all personal godliness."

– William Carey

Time Well Spent
– Colin Webster,
Alpha

Jesus told his friends to pray for more workers to spread the good news (Matt 9:38) and he prayed himself when he saw a glimpse of his world wide ministry (John 12:27–28). He also spent time in prayer before he was betrayed (John 17). Jesus had a real assurance that his prayers were always heard (John 11:41) for which he was thankful (Luke 10:21). He prayed protection for his followers (John 17:11) and he prayed for us (John 17:20).

His prayers expressed a consuming desire that the Father be glorified (John 12:28). Jesus' best known prayer may be his agonising, urgent intercession in the Garden of Gethsemane (Matt 26:36–46).

"During the days of Jesus' life on earth, he offered up prayers and petitions with loud cries and tears to the one who could save him from death, and he was heard because of his reverent submission."

– Heb 5:7

A new Christian asks you to give them some helpful hints on prayer. What practical guidelines and ideas can you offer?

Less is more: fasting

Fasting can be particularly valuable when it is practised in community, with the whole church family being invited to participate.

John's gospel does not actually mention that Jesus fasted, although Jesus did state his sense of priority in John, saying that he had meat to eat that his disciples did not know about (John 4:32–34). We know from the other three gospel writers that fasting was his practice (Luke 4:2).

Prayer: Finding the Heart's True Home
– Richard Foster,
Harper San Francisco

Fasting introduces the idea of us being in control and dominion over the body rather than vice versa (Luke 12:33; Phil 3:19; Rom 16:18; 1 Cor 6:13). Jesus assumed that those who followed him would practice fasting; he says *when* you fast, not *if* (Matt 16:24).

Although fasting is generally related to food, it may be that married

JESUS AND THE FATHER IN JOHN

John's gospel particularly focuses on the relationship between Jesus and his Father. He and the Father working together (John 5:19), he comes in the Father's name (John 5:43) and the Father draws people to the Son (John 6:44). He lived because of the Father (John 6:57), and now those that know him know the Father also (John 8:19).

No-one comes to the Father but by Jesus (John 14:6) and those that love Jesus are loved by the Father (John 14:21). Ultimately Jesus would return to the father (John 13:1) having drank the cup that the Father gave him (John 18:11).

TWISTING GOD'S ARM

The book of Acts describes a failed attempt by a group who tried to get God on their side by manipulative fasting: "The next morning the Jews formed a conspiracy and bound themselves with an oath not to eat or drink until they had killed Paul. ... They went to the chief priests and elders and said, 'We have taken a solemn oath not to eat anything until we have killed Paul...'." (Acts 23:12,14). We are never told what happened to these zealots – but their prayer obviously was unsuccessful.

Using fasting in a manipulative way was attempted in Jeremiah's day too. God said, "Although they fast, I will not listen to their cry; though they offer burnt offerings and grain offerings, I will not accept them. Instead, I will destroy them with the sword, famine and plague" (Jer 14:12). Fasting didn't move God at all.

Fasting is not a spiritualised hunger strike designed to force God's hand. He is good (Psalm 119:8) and eager to answer our prayers. He is generous (James 1:5) and keen to give us 'good gifts' (Matt 7:11).

couples decide to abstain from sexual relationships for a season, in order that they may give themselves fully to dedicated prayer (1 Cor 7:5). This is not to imply that there is anything 'unspiritual' about the wholly proper celebration of our sexuality within marriage – any more than eating food or drinking water is unspiritual. Dietrich Bonhoeffer said, 'The essence of chastity is not the suppression of lust but the total orientation of one's life towards a goal.' Other examples of fasting are abstinence from alcohol, television and other elements of life, which putting aside for a while will allow us to focus single-mindedly on God.

Fasting, like all the disciplines, should not be the focus of our attention – and fasting is one of the disciplines that seems to demand attention for itself, with a growling stomach to remind us of our supposed devotion. It is not to be conducted in a spirit of self-righteous sadness, because it will ultimately be a source of joy to us – and any attempt to advertise our 'piety' is hypocrisy (Matt 6:16–18).

Fasting is denying my self. It is denying not only my body, but also my wants. It is a way of saying that food and my desires are secondary to something else. Fasting is afflicting one's soul – an act of self-denial. But it is far more than that, and this is where the monks and hermits went wrong.

Biblical fasting is always coupled with prayer.

Biblical fasting is not eating with a spiritual goal in mind. Biblical fasting always occurs together with prayer in the Bible – **always**. You can pray without fasting, but you cannot fast without praying. Biblical fasting is deliberately abstaining from food for a spiritual reason, goal, or purpose.

NOTE: *Common sense demands that we be cautious about advocating this practice without being aware of the dangerous diseases of anorexia and bulimia, or where individuals may be particularly vulnerable – children, pregnant women and diabetics, for example.*

Stop the world: solitude and silence

Life is busy, frantic even, and extremely noisy. Some of us gain a sense of security from our crammed diaries – if we are in demand, then we must be important. If we receive lots of mail, it must be a sign of our station in the world that so many feel the need to be in contact with us. And with e-mail, faxes and mobile phones, we are in danger of creating technology that fosters an epidemic of superficiality. Petrol stations are now installing televisions in the pumps so

"Refrain from gluttony and thou shalt the more easily restrain all the inclinations of the flesh."
– Thomas à Kempis

FASTING LINKS
www.fasting.com
www.fastingprayer.com
www.ccci.org/howtofast

"Yet even now," says the Lord, "return to me with all your heart, with fasting..."
– *Joel 2:12*

"Eating – particularly eating out – used to be centred around family and friendship; it was a social event rather than just the filling of the bag within us called the stomach. The advent of fast-food/drive-through culture has robbed eating of its warmth, and rendered it to be a loveless mechanism, a topping up of self in the hurry to get on to the next thing."
– *Jeff Lucas*

"Fasting helps to express, to deepen, and to confirm the resolution that we are ready to sacrifice anything – to sacrifice ourselves – to attain what we seek for the kingdom of God."
– *Andrew Murray*

GUIDELINES FOR FASTING

The Bible mentions three types of fasting:

Normal Fast: Water only. For as long as the individual or group feels led. Jesus fasted for 40 days (Matt 4:2). The more common practice of a normal fast appears to be from one to three days.

Partial Fast: Restricted eating. Daniel, Shadrack, Meshach and Abednego; eating only vegetables and drinking only water (Dan 1:15). Daniel practised a partial fast for three weeks (Dan 10:3).

Absolute Fast: No food or water. Not to exceed three days. Exceptions to this three-day limit (1 Kings 19:8; Deut 9:9–18 and Exod 34:28) were based upon direct, divine guidance and care. Moses (Deut 9:9–18 and Exod 34:28); Elijah (1 Kings 19:8); Ezra (Ezra 10:6); Esther and her household (Esther 4:16); and Paul (Acts 9:9).

Fasting is voluntary

Fasting was thought of so highly in the Early Church they inserted the word 'fasting' into the Bible even though it isn't in the original manuscripts (see various translations or margin notes for Matt 17:21; Mark 9:29; Acts 10:30; 1 Cor 7:5). This emphasis caused them to repeat the mistake of the Pharisees and prescribe days for fasting: twice a week, on Wednesday and Friday.

A set day for fasting is commanded in Scripture only once – on the Day of Atonement (Lev 16). This was connected with a deep mournful spirit in confessing sin. Jesus is our atonement offering, so we don't need to observe the Day of Atonement, and nowhere else in all the Bible does Scripture command fasting at a specific time or on a specific occasion.

A Christian should fast only when they feel the Spirit of God leading them to fast. It is a totally voluntary decision, though there may be times when those in authority over us proclaim a fast, as was done by Saul in 1 Sam 14:24 or Jehoshaphat in 2 Chron 20:3.

A fast was usually for one day (as in Jdg 20:26; 1 Sam 14:24; 2 Sam 1:12; 3:35) from sunrise to sunset, and then after sundown food would be taken. The Biblical principle here is that the length of time you fast is determined by your own desires and the occasion or purpose of the fast. There is freedom in the Lord here.

In the Bible, fasting often occurs as something you do while carrying on your everyday activities. Matt 6:16–18 demonstrates this, since Jesus pictures a situation in which Christians are among other people going about their normal duties and activities. In fact, soldiers involved in the activity of warfare sometimes fasted (1 Sam 14:24) as well as the sailors on ship with Paul (Acts 27:33). There is a certain sense in which fasting, even in the midst of your daily activities, becomes a constant prayer to the Lord.

A PHYSICIAN'S NOTE: Make sure you are medically able to fast before attempting it.

Begin with short fasts and gradually move to longer periods if you desire. Don't start with a three day fast.

Be prepared for some dizziness, headache, or nausea. Most of our bodies have never gone without food for longer than a few hours.

Break a long fast gradually with meals that are light and easy to digest.

Mix your fast with prayer, Bible reading, singing or devotional reading. Remember: fasting is not an end in itself. Seek the Lord, not the experience of fasting. Keep checking your motives concerning your fasts. Hypocrisy and spiritual pride can easily creep in. There is a reward for fasting, but only fasting done with the right motives (Matt 23:28).

God's Chosen Fast – Arthur Wallis, Kingsway

"You can pray without fasting, but you cannot fast without praying."

The Hidden Power of Prayer and Fasting – Mahesh Chavda, Word

"Retirement is the laboratory of the spirit; interior solitude and silence are its two wings. All great works are prepared in the desert, including the redemption of the world. The precursors, the followers, the Master himself, all obeyed or have to obey one and the same law. Prophets, apostles, preachers, martyrs, pioneers of knowledge, inspired artists in every art, ordinary men and the Man God, all pay tribute to loneliness, to the life of silence, to the night."

– A.G. Sertillanges, The Intellectual Life

that we can be assailed with advertising while filling the tank. Even a thirty second wait on a telephone is filled with *muzak* so that we will not have to 'endure' silence.

Jesus was often hounded by crowds. But he took time to commune with his father, to think, to order his inner life, to prepare for times of great trial and pressure. He knew what it is to 'be still… and know God' (Psalm 46:10). And he commended Mary's desire to be still and listen to him over Martha's bustling, hurried hospitality. Upon hearing the news of the death of John the Baptist, he withdrew to a lonely place apart (Matt 14:23).

Peter is a portrait of activism in John's gospel – study the lives of Peter and John and you'll see that John always understands before Peter, and Peter always acts before John. Jesus took time to reflect in quietness.

Our call is to 'contemplative activism'. This may be busy, but it will refuse breathless superficiality – and that will demand solitude and silence. This solitude is not just an escape from people, but rather a deliberate drawing aside in order to 'cling to Christ'. Not an emptiness, but an abstaining from human company so that we can focus on friendship with our Lord.

It may be that we should seek to build in a guided or lone retreat, or a day or two away on our own. We must also recognise that this will be impossible for some.

Hermits are not just characters confined to history: well known writer Brennan Manning undertook an extraordinary adventure into solitude, living in a cave for a whole winter.

Other uses of solitude can be:

- **'Mini' sabbaths** – minutes or hours alone – the quantity of time not being the main factor. Ten minutes of quiet, perhaps in the smallest room of the house, is better than nothing.
- **The night watch** – why not occasionally set the alarm to wake you in the middle of the night for half an hour, so that you can sit alone and quietly reflect, or give thanks, or just be with God without any sense of intense prayer?
- **'Waking the dawn'** – Jesus was in the habit of getting up early to pray. There is nothing intrinsically special or 'holy' about getting up in the early hours of the day, except that they are usually a quieter period, and you can focus your attention on

PEACE SO GREAT

The great holy men, where they might, fled men's fellowship and chose to live with God in secret places. One said: "As I was among men I came back a less man, that is to say less holy... . If in the beginning of thy conversion thou keep thy cell and dwell well therein it shall be to thee afterwards as a dear and well beloved friend and most pleasant solace. In silence and quiet the devout soul profiteth and learneth the secrets of the scriptures... . Leave vain things to the vain... . Shut thy door upon thee and call to thee Jesu thy love: dwell with him in thy cell for thou shalt not find elsewhere so great peace..."
– *Thomas à Kempis, The Imitation of Christ*

MODERN CAVEMAN MANNING

In the winter of 1968 to 1969, I lived in a cave in the mountains of the Zaragosa Desert in Spain. For seven months I saw no one, never heard the sound of a human voice. Hewn out of the face of the mountain, the cave towered six thousand feet above sea level. Each Sunday morning a brother from the village of Farlete below dropped off food, drinking water, and kerosene at a designated spot. Within the cave a stone partition divided the chapel on the right from the living quarters on the left. A stone slab covered with potato sacks served as a bed. The other furniture was a rugged granite desk, a wooden chair, a Sterno stove, and a kerosene lamp. On the wall of the chapel hung a three-foot crucifix. I awoke each morning at 2am and went into the chapel for an hour of nocturnal adoration.

On the night of December 13, during what began as a long and lonely hour of prayer, I heard in faith Jesus Christ say; "For love of you I left my Father's side. I came to you who ran from me, fled me, who did not want to hear my name. For love of you I was covered with spit, punched, beaten, and affixed to the wood of the cross."

These words are burned on my life. Whether I am in a state of grace or disgrace, elation or depression, that night of fire quietly burns on... I realized that no man has ever loved me and no one ever could love me as he did. I went out of the cave, stood on the precipice, and shouted into the darkness, "Jesus, are you crazy? Are you out of your mind to have loved me so much?" I learned that night what a wise old man had told me years earlier: "Only the one who has experienced it can know what the love of Jesus Christ is. Once you have experienced it, nothing else in the world will seem more beautiful or desirable." – *Brennan Manning, The Signature of Jesus*

God before the working business of the day begins.

- **Walks in the city or the country**. Travel used to be at a far slower pace – it would take days or weeks to take a journey that we could cover in breathless hours. Why not take up walking a couple of times a week – and if you decide not to walk alone, then why not use part of the time for a mutually agreed silence?

Make a conscious decision to be more thoughtful about your speech and commit yourself to listening more – particularly when you are 'sharing your faith', which is not meant to be an inspired monologue.

Turn the television/radio off for a while.

"It is not easy to be solitary unless you are born ruthless."
– Jessamyn West

"Jesus... withdrew again to a mountain by himself."
– John 6:15

"After leaving them, he went up onto a mountainside to pray..."
– Mark 6:46

"People who love one another can be silent together."
– Eberhard Arnold

? **It must have been simple for people in bygone days to be quiet or go on a retreat. It's just impossible and impractical for us millennium three people. Do you agree?**

? **What is the difference between loneliness and solitude? Which do you experience more?**

"Slow to speak."
– James 1:19

Fame: the disciplines of secrecy, sacrifice and servanthood

Jesus in John's gospel exemplifies the heart of the servant as he girds himself with a towel, and washes the sweaty, dirty feet of his friends – and his betrayer, Judas. He refused to advertise his goodness, but often told people to keep the miracle that they had experienced to themselves – not only because wide publicity would have frustrated his messianic purposes but also because he allowed the Father to handle his public relations.

Serving and giving are not enough – pride is always lurking at the door, wanting us to do our giving and our serving in the place where others can see it. This was the snare that the Pharisees had fallen into (Matt 23). The same is true of prayer – much of which needs to be done in secret (Matt 6:6). This does not mean that we can never engage in coordinated, public times of prayer (as some have suggested, calling for 'closet' prayer only) but rather that we must discipline ourselves to avoid advertising our commitment.

"He that seeketh no outward witness for himself, it appeareth openly that he hath committed himself all wholly to God."
– Thomas à Kempis

REDEEM THE CHANCE MOMENTS

"You must learn ... to make good use of chance moments, when waiting for someone, when going from place to place, or when in society where to be a good listener is all that is required; ... at such times it is easy to lift the heart to God, and thereby gain fresh strength for further duties. The less time one has the more carefully it should be managed. If you wait for free, convenient seasons in which to fulfil real duties, you run the risk of waiting forever; especially in such a life as yours. No, make use of chance moments... ." – *Francois Fenelon, Spiritual Letters to Women*

LOOK AT ME, I'M SO SPIRITUAL...

In Jesus' time fasting was an important part of the Jewish life. The Pharisees fasted twice a week (Luke 18:12a).

The Talmud tells us that this was on the 2nd and 5th day (Monday and Thursday). Why those days? According to the Pharisees it was because Moses went up on Mt. Sinai to get the Law on the fifth day and returned on the second. At least, that's what they said.

But if you look closely into Jewish history, you find another possible reason for the Pharisees fasting on Monday and Thursday – market day in the city of Jerusalem was on the second and fifth day. Everyone from the countryside came to town on those days. It was on these two days that the Pharisees chose to hold their fasts. They would walk through the streets with their hair dishevelled; they would put on old clothes and cover themselves with dirt; they would cover their faces with white chalk in order to look pale; and they would dump ashes over their head as a sign of their humility. Fasting had become a "look at how spiritual I am" exercise. It was a hypocrisy.

Do you think we should have 'foot washing' services – or is something else being taught by Jesus about servanthood?

The church project you worked on very, very hard has now been completed – and no-one has thanked you. Do you say anything? Shouldn't the rest of the community be learning how to encourage? And if you stay silent, will that lesson ever be learned?

We have to party – celebration and fellowship

God is happy. He brings news of joy (Luke 2:10), and comes to us 'that our joy might be full' (John 15:11). God has gifts like food, sex, music, friendship, and laughter for our enjoyment. Jesus began his ministry in the warmth of family celebration at Cana (John 2) and enjoyed the fun of a party so much that he was falsely accused of being a 'drunkard' (Matt 11:19, Luke 7:34).

He told stories which were very humorous – the joke of trying to get a camel through the eye of a needle (Matt 19:24) is largely lost on us, but that's to do with culture and humour. Children were drawn to him in a very open and natural way, and children don't tend to like being around wide eyed, staring ascetics. He was a popular party guest, and not just because of his incredible gift of wine provision.

"The Christian should be an alleluia from head to foot!"

– Augustine of Hippo

So how is fellowship and fun a discipline? It is a needed choice that we may need to make when

- we are tired and would rather just avoid people
- when others in our church have irritated or offended us and we are tempted to beat a hasty retreat
- when we have been raised in a joyless Christianity which has sadly taught us to be nervous of laughter, thinking it to be 'unspiritual'.

"Man's celebrative and imaginative faculties have atrophied."

– Harvey Cox

Some steps to take:

- Recognise the spirituality of a whole hearted party. If you're in doubt, watch a Jewish celebration.
- Realise that laughter is very good for you. Laugh at yourself, and enjoy good, wholesome comedy. Risque comedy is a desecration of genuine, God breathed fun.
- Encourage colour and creativity in your corporate gatherings. One church has an artists easel set out in their public meetings so that those who feel more comfortable expressing their wor-

FOOD IS GOOD

Food is good – it is for our sustenance (Gen 1:30) and meant to be enjoyed (Ecc 2:24–25; 5:18). Eating, from a biblical perspective, is intended to be more than just the recharging of our fuel tanks.

Gen 18:1–8 gives us one of the first examples of fellowship and food. All through the Old Testament the people of God came together for fellowship over food. God made food for fellowship. He even commanded that some of the sacrifices offered to him at the temple were to be shared with others. These were communal meals – meals in which the whole community sat down and ate together (Deut 12:6,7,18). Families still find a resource of love, fellowship, discussion, and understanding when they come together to eat.

ship in paint or sculpture can engage more fully during corporate worship times.

- Make memories with friends and family. Find little reasons to celebrate, and establish some traditions.
- Thankfulness is more than 'saying grace' at meal times. Practice the art of living gratitude.
- Redeem the celebrations of our culture. Make a big party out of Easter and Christmas. Invite neighbours in for cheese and wine, and not just to 'evangelise' them.

Restoring your Spiritual Passion – Gordon MacDonald, Highland Books

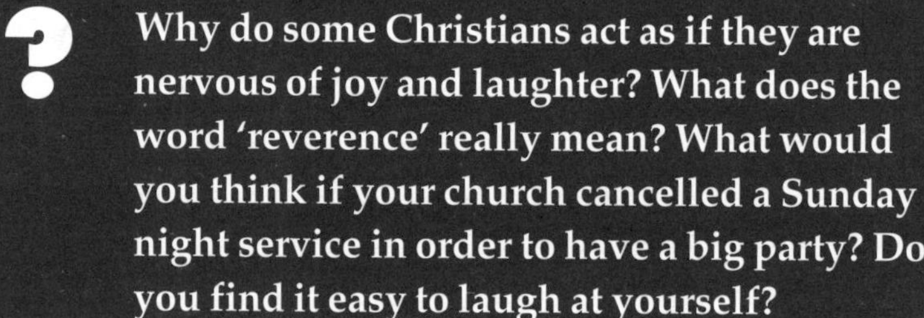
Why do some Christians act as if they are nervous of joy and laughter? What does the word 'reverence' really mean? What would you think if your church cancelled a Sunday night service in order to have a big party? Do you find it easy to laugh at yourself?

A lesson from today's world

The Drugs and Discipleship Dilemma

Christian discipleship means caring for those who need care.

Throughout John's gospel, Jesus encourages his disciples to care for the poor, needy and suffering (John 5:1–9; 6:5–10; 9:1–7; 11:1–44). Very often, Christians say that they do not know what to do for a drug user or drug addict, but there is a huge amount that any Christian can do. By simply befriending someone, we can express Christian love and care. Also remember that being a Christian and caring for someone does not mean that you have to be a doormat.

Christi-Anarchy – Dave Andrews, Hodder & Stoughton

Discipleship is not always an easy road, but when we understand that through all the hard talking, Jesus loved everyone so much more than we could imagine, we cannot fail to see the wonderful combination of love and discipline in his teaching.

Christian discipleship can prevent drug abuse (young disciples take note).

A survey conducted by the Evangelical Coalition on Drugs (ECOD) at Spring Harvest 1995 found that young people are "significantly less likely to engage in illicit drug use when positively engaged in a Christian walk."

URBAN EXPRESSION

Urban Expression is a new venture – started in late 1997 – run jointly by Oasis Trust and Spurgeon's College. Its aim is to recruit, equip, deploy and support self-financing teams which will pioneer innovative and relevant expressions of the Christian church in under-churched areas of the inner city.

Church planting is something of a fashion amongst some Christians in the UK at the moment. Everyone is reading about it or going to conferences about it. Those involved with Urban Expression are also getting on with the task of doing it. Looking at needy under-churched areas in inner cities, Urban Expression recognises that traditional church planting models (for example, the mother-daughter model) will not always work. Urban Expression is a brave attempt to model something new and different with a readiness to learn and make mistakes along the way.

Each team is built around a team leader or leaders (eg a married couple). Team leaders shape the team's work and usually already have a track record of effective leadership in similar situations.

There are no funds provided for any member of an Urban Expression team, not even the leader. Some members may choose to work full time, seeing their work situation as their mission ground and their income as a resource to be shared by the team. Others may choose to work part-time, and others may raise the necessary income through a network of supporters in order to give all of their time to the community or to part-time study. Teams work their finances in many different ways, with some of them choosing to pool all their money into a common purse; creativity, generosity and openness are the guidelines.

Team members come with different skills and abilities, and not everyone needs to be an evangelist. The emphasis is on using the gifts of each member of the team and to work closely together. Teams will not have a blueprint of a perfect urban church to work from. They will be involved in a process of discovering what church should look like in their community. Therefore, team members must be people who enjoy rediscovering from the Bible what church is all about, who take this task responsibly and who will feel secure in the insecurity of not always knowing the answers.

The values of Urban Expression give each of the teams a great deal of freedom but define the following clear guidelines:-

We will be humble

We are on a journey of discovery trying to find ways of being church that are relevant in the inner city. We want to learn from others and, above all, to recognise our complete dependence on God.

We will experiment

We will try alternative ways of communicating the good news and being church, not for the sake of the alternative, but because we recognise that so many people remain unreached by the gospel that we must take the responsibility to investigate other ways of communicating it. We understand the risk of failure, but will be committed to trying anyway.

We will empower

We are committed to releasing local people into the calling God has for them and will not impose our ideas, but will seek to learn from and encourage local new Christians in their understanding of God.

We will resource

Urban churches use all they have in the task of witnessing to their faith. We will not drain them of even more resources, but will commit ourselves to being a resource to them.

Accountability is also an important part of the Urban Expression philosophy, with team members accountable to the team leader and the team leader in turn accountable to a coordinator.

A number of things may account for this:

- When someone is walking closely with God, they don't need any other 'buzz' (Psa 119:57, Phil 4:19).
- The true disciple understands the first commandment: "You shall have no other gods before me" (Exod 20:3). Any drug addict can tell you that drugs soon become an idol, the sole focus of attention or a life-dominating issue – a god by any other name.
- The true disciple wears the armour of God (Eph 6:10–18) and is able to resist the ever-present 'flaming arrows' of the evil one – often felt in the form of peer pressure.

"The thief comes only to steal and kill and destroy; I have come that they may have life, and have it to the full."

– John 10:10

Being a disciple is not about living by a list of don'ts – it is about living an abundant life rather than a deficient and unfulfilled one (John 10:10).

Being a disciple of Jesus Christ is the only way to true freedom from all life-controlling problems.

There is a growing body of evidence showing that former addicts who undergo a programme of Christian rehabilitation and become true disciples of Jesus Christ, have a much better chance of staying drug free than those who do not. This will come as no surprise to those who know that our Lord can free us from any bondage.

Unfortunately, some people mistakenly believe that once you are 'off' drugs, all your problems are over. The reality is, however, that there are always fundamental issues in the life of the addict that need long-term healing.

Discipleship, for the addict and the non-addict alike, takes the same path. Jesus understood the concept of taking time to deal with fundamental issues in a person's life. See in John's gospel how he took Simon Peter through a journey of challenge, discipline, change, and renewal (compare John 18:15–27, with John 21:3–4, 9, 15–17).

Some issues that are common to discipleship and recovery from addiction:

- "All have sinned and fall short of the glory of God" (Rom 3:23, John 8:34–36).
- We need to ask for God's forgiveness (1 John 1:9).
- We all need to face up to the wrongs done to us, and not try to bury them, either by using drugs or keeping a stiff upper lip (Matt 18:21–35).

JESUS THE DISCIPLER

The most common areas of hurt that recovering addicts have to work through are rejection, grief, insecurity, emotional abuse, physical abuse, sexual abuse, and spiritual abuse.

You don't have to have been a drug addict to have experienced any or all of these, however. You may have found ways of coping with these hurts other than through an 'obvious' addiction. An eating disorder or dependence on a prescription drug is less 'antisocial' than addiction to an illegal drug, but similar issues are often at the root. Some people will use other behaviours to distract themselves from these hurts – work, sex, sport, religion or controlling other people.

We all need to forgive those who have wronged us (Luke 11:4, John 20:23, Matt 6:15, Eph 4:32). To forgive someone is to release them from our judgement, or to relinquish our 'right' to get even (Matt 7:1–2, Lev 19:18).

We all need to submit ourselves to God's rule. This means turning our backs on rebellion and making him Lord of all in our lives (Gal 2:20, Rom 6:11–14; 8:9–17).

A lesson from Jesus

John provides us with a vivid portrait of the beloved disciple in his gospel – a useful model of discipleship for us to consider. Argument has simmered over the years about his identity – he is traditionally identified as John himself.

John's gospel highlights key character traits of the closest friend and disciple of Jesus, 'the one whom Jesus loved' (John 13:23, 20:2).

He loved being with and close to Jesus. In John 13 he reclines next to Jesus – John uses identical terminology to describe Jesus' relationship 'at the Father's side' (John 1:18).

He is faithful to Jesus under pressure, being present at the trial, where he was 'known to the high priest' (John 18:15) and at the cross, where he was the only one of the disciples present – the only one of them to witness Jesus' death (John 19:26).

He was entrusted with high responsibility, being asked to take care of Jesus' mother, Mary (John 19:26).

He was entrusted with revelation and insight – first at the empty tomb. John always understands before Peter – and Peter always

takes action before John. Consider the boat scene in John 21. John realises that it is Jesus who is the stranger on the shore – and Peter jumps straight out of the boat in order to get to Jesus. John was the first to believe in the risen Lord (John 20:3,8).

The beloved disciple is regarded in John's gospel as the ideal disciple of Jesus – his relationship with Jesus was one of loving intimacy. And in that relationship, discipleship as relational is seen most clearly – for a disciple of Jesus not only believes in Jesus, but remains in his love.

SECTION 3

JESUS THE EVANGELIST

"We call upon every bishop, diocese and congregation to see their primary task is to share in and show the love of God in Jesus Christ and to continue the work of evangelism beyond the Decade of Evangelism."
– General Synod 1999 of the Church of England

"Most evangelism training involves helping people learn how to 'say the words' of the gospel. Little attention is paid to developing a biblical philosophy of ministry which moves the corporate life of the church away from ugliness to beauty. The best argument for Christianity is Christians; their joy ... their completeness. But the strongest argument against Christianity is also Christians – when they are sombre and joyless, when they are self-righteous and smug in complacent consecration, when they are narrow and repressive – then Christianity dies a thousand deaths."
– Joe Aldrich

"Next Sunday there will be more people in church in Moscow than in London."
– Alan Walker

SECTION 3

JESUS THE EVANGELIST

BIBLE PASSAGE

John 4:4–26

Now he had to go through Samaria. 5So he came to a town in Samaria called Sychar, near the plot of
ground Jacob had given to his son Joseph. 6Jacob's well was there, and Jesus, tired as he was from the
journey, sat down by the well. It was about the sixth hour.

7When a Samaritan woman came to draw water, Jesus said to her, "Will you give me a drink?" 8(His
disciples had gone into the town to buy food.)

9The Samaritan woman said to him, "You are a Jew and I am a Samaritan woman. How can you ask me
for a drink?" (For Jews do not associate with Samaritans.)

10Jesus answered her, "If you knew the gift of God and who it is that asks you for a drink, you would
have asked him and he would have given you living water."

11"Sir," the woman said, "you have nothing to draw with and the well is deep. Where can you get this
living water? 12Are you greater than our father Jacob, who gave us the well and drank from it himself, as
did also his sons and his flocks and herds?"

13Jesus answered, "Everyone who drinks this water will be thirsty again, 14but whoever drinks the water
I give him will never thirst. Indeed, the water I give him will become in him a spring of water welling up
to eternal life."

15The woman said to him, "Sir, give me this water so that I won't get thirsty and have to keep coming
here to draw water."

16He told her, "Go, call your husband and come back."

17"I have no husband," she replied.

Jesus said to her, "You are right when you say you have no husband. 18The fact is, you have had five
husbands, and the man you now have is not your husband. What you have just said is quite true."

19"Sir," the woman said, "I can see that you are a prophet. 20Our fathers worshipped on this mountain,
but you Jews claim that the place where we must worship is in Jerusalem."

21Jesus declared, "Believe me, woman, a time is coming when you will worship the Father neither on this
mountain nor in Jerusalem. 22You Samaritans worship what you do not know; we worship what we do
know, for salvation is from the Jews. 23Yet a time is coming and has now come when the true worshippers will worship the Father in spirit and truth, for they are the kind of worshippers the Father seeks.
24God is spirit, and his worshippers must worship in spirit and in truth."

25The woman said, "I know that Messiah" (called Christ) "is coming. When he comes, he will explain
everything to us."

26Then Jesus declared, "I who speak to you am he."

Comment

v5 Divine appointments?

The inconvenience of evangelism

v6 'He was tired ... and sat down'

v9 A heart for the marginalised

v10–15 Water and life

v18–20 Confrontation and evasion

v21–24 A glorious anticipation.

NOTES

JESUS THE EVANGELIST

Lord, we don't know where you are going, so how can we know the way? Jesus answered, I am the way and the truth and the life. No one comes to the Father except through me. John 14:5

When the two disciples heard him say this, they followed Jesus. John 1:37

A great crowd of people followed him because they saw the miraculous signs he had performed. John 6:2

Jesus answered, "The work of God is this: to believe in the one he has sent." John 6:29

Everyone who listens to the Father and learns from him comes to me. John 6:45

Even as he spoke, many put their faith in him. John 8:30

Whoever serves me must follow me; John 12:26

JESUS THE EVANGELIST – MENU

The word 'banquet' creates an image of splendid grandeur … an exclusive feast for the invited, for the privileged few only… . But Jesus taught something entirely different about his kind of party, commanding his followers to issue invitations to whoever would come, and calling on them to 'go out quickly into the streets and alleys' and invite the poor and the marginalised to come to an eternal feast (Luke 14:15–24).

Of course, the Jesus approach to banqueting upset the Pharisees, who thought that the dining table was a kind of 'little temple' at which one only worshipped with the righteous.

We ponder in this section the fact that Jesus has called the Church to be a community of proclamation, incarnation and welcome – not an internally focused, ghettoised group who 'get fed' every Sunday while those around them starve for reality and truth. We consider the dreaded word 'evangelism' – what is our mission, what is our message? And we look at our methods – are they effective, biblical and Jesus-centred?

THE INVITATION

THE INVITATION

Following Jesus involves evangelism

Christianity without evangelism would need to jettison its very foundations.

- Evangelism is so clearly Christian.

Announcing the good news

Much of Jesus' ministry was spent announcing the good news of the kingdom of God. He modelled evangelism, trained his disciples in evangelism, sent them out to evangelise, rejoiced over those who received their message, promised the Holy Spirit to empower their evangelism and left them with a call to evangelise the whole world ringing in their ears.

The New Testament is a mission document, set in the context of vibrant evangelism and church planting.

- There is good news to share. And church at its best is very good indeed. Most Christians deep down do want to share their faith and talk about Jesus.
- There is a growing interest in spirituality.

Growing interest in spirituality

The secular world view stemming from the Enlightenment has not proved adequate. Materialism still attracts people, but satisfies fewer. Concern for the environment, experiments with alternative lifestyles and hunger for spiritual experiences are evident.

Neither atheistic communism nor consumerist capitalism have been able to provide permanent distractions. There is a resurgent interest in the occult, in New Age spirituality and in the older alternatives offered by Islamic, Buddhist and Hindu communities now resident in Europe. This should be a fertile environment for evangelism if only we can discover how to engage in this in ways that engage creatively with our society.

Most Christians – and most non-Christians – would agree that they do not like evangelism.

Many Christians feel that they ought to be evangelising their society, and most are very uncomfortable about it.

book.link

Lost For Words – James Lawrence, The Bible Reading Fellowship

Evangelism – How-To Guide – Administry

"Jesus never met a prostitute – he met a person."

COMMON WORD ASSOCIATION RESPONSES:

evangelical – fundamentalist, right-wing, middle class, moral majority, closed minded, intolerant, Bible-bashing;

evangelist – manipulator, showman, dishonest, after your money, powerful personality, eloquent speaker, Billy Graham;

evangelism – being preached at in the open air, being accosted by a zealous stranger, texts on posters, hype, pressure, emotional hysteria, embarrassment, invitations to church events, crusades.

"There was a part of me that secretly felt evangelism was something you shouldn't do to your dog, let alone a friend."

– Rebecca Manley Pippert

Challenges to evangelism

Negative word associations

The British press frequently use the word 'evangelical' interchangeably with the word 'evangelist' – and for many, both words have developed negative connotations.

Contemporary influences

Evangelism has a bad name not only because of past practices and assumptions but because of the ways in which it is still being practised.

Nor is the problem merely stylistic. The message of 'good news' that is proclaimed in much contemporary evangelism often appears to be neither news nor good.

- Too often it fails to address contemporary concerns.
- Sometimes it makes assumptions about its hearers that are unwarranted – for example, that unchurched people are irreligious, morally bankrupt, or philosophical geniuses.
- It presents a pre-packaged, privatised gospel, embodies establishment values and middle-class morality and appears to be little more than a desperate recruiting drive for a declining institution.
- The churches, which are meant to be communities that incarnate this good news, are often perceived as riddled with hypocrisy, racism, sexism, materialism and backbiting.

How to Reach Secular People – George Hunter III, Abingdon

Little wonder that those who are Christian, and those who are not, find evangelism unattractive. And no surprise that suggestions have been made for a worldwide moratorium on evangelism. Sensitive and thinking Christians struggle to know how to redeem this situation.

First steps

We need to avoid – and encourage others to avoid – any activities that will further endorse the negative image of evangelism, by thinking through the impact of our evangelistic methods much more carefully.

- We need to work hard at establishing or restoring the credibility of the local church as a community of good news.
- We need to take care that we do not confuse resistance to evangelism with resistance to the gospel. If our approach is not working, don't blame others.

"The depths of people's ignorance on central aspects of the Christian faith is almost unfathomable."

– Anthony King in The Daily Telegraph, *31 December, 1999*

NEGATIVE HISTORICAL FACTORS FOR EVANGELISM:

The use of force to spread the gospel – baptisms at sword point, use of imperial power in mission.

The use of bribery to spread the gospel – "rice Christians", social acceptability for Christians, favourable treatment by authorities.

Anti-Semitism – in Constantine's time all *except* Jews were considered Christian.

The imposition of Western culture – in mission models, denigration or demonisation of other cultures. Black Africans going to church meetings in white European dress, singing non-African music, etc.

SPECIFIC PROBLEMS INCLUDE:

- Oddballs, charlatans, manipulators – as portrayed by Steve Martin in the 1992 film 'Leap of Faith' – and sadly, in real life by some ministries.
- Outdated language, inappropriate methods and the use of terminology that almost beggars belief in its insensitivity (such as crusades to reach Muslims).
- Failure to embody the good news through service and seeking justice – evangelism reduced to information about the gospel rather than relevant demonstration of the gospel.
- Failure to appreciate fears and sensitivities in a multicultural environment.

Some of the material in this section is taken from Chris Thackery's book *Epidemic of Life*, published by Word.

Epidemic of Life – Chris Thackery, Word

"Much of evangelism is based on the assumption that we are still living in the middle ages."

– Lord Soper

- We need to demonstrate a new humility in evangelism – being bold but sensitive, asking questions as well as giving answers.
- We need to ask some basic questions about evangelism.

Our mission

Firstly, we need to look at the culture surrounding those we are trying to reach.

Britain – a post-Christian culture

As we saw in Section One, there were enormous consequences of the conversion of Constantine and the declaration of Christianity as Rome's official religion.

Church structures became central to social organisation, judicial systems and education. Church doctrines not only defined the spiritual values of society but even determined the framework for morality, science and the arts. Christian values provided the baseline, however badly understood or complied with.

This whole edifice, Christendom, has been under pressure for quite some time, but has shown signs of crumbling much more rapidly in the last 100 years. Our globalized, multiracial society no longer accepts Christianity as the default and this has major implications.

- Negatively, the destructive effects on society as it progressively deviates from biblical principles of healthy living seem likely to get worse before they improve. This is not, of course, to underplay the many individuals and Christian organisations working faithfully to promote biblical principles and values in our society.
- Positively, an emerging population that is largely ignorant of Christianity may prove easier to evangelise than one that is subject to misconception and negative associations. And perhaps the Church has a new opportunity to develop an identity that is clearly distinct from the establishment. It's an opportunity to become a radical counter-culture of the first century model.

Secularism – the revival

According to Os Guinness, since 1900 the percentage of the world's atheistic and non-religious peoples has grown from 0.2 per cent to 21.3 per cent – in other words, from less than one-fifth of one per cent to over one-fifth of the world's population. This is the most dramatic change on the entire religious map of the 20th century.

THREE MYTHS ABOUT SECULAR, 'UNCHURCHED' PEOPLE

How have 500 years of secularisation changed society? What can we know about secular people that helps our Christian witness? What are our points of contact with them, and strategies for reaching them? There are three widely held beliefs about secular people that are untrue.

False Belief 1

Some pundits claim secularisation has erased all religious consciousness. And we are entering an age of 'no religion'.

Not so. Western culture today, Ken Chafin says, is much like Athens when (Acts 17) Paul reasoned with people – influenced by a range of religions and philosophies. We have the modern versions and a range of others from astrology to Zen, while new religions continue to surface. In the early 1970s a 17-year-old guru led a religious movement that seemed to some the wave of the future. The late 1980s saw the New Age movement. Other examples include the deification of the state (as in Nazi Germany); the deification of a political ideology (as in Marxism); and the deification of a culture (as in Japanese Shinto and the American way of life). There is extensive evidence that people are incurably religious, but attend church services less often, and pick and choose religious fragments at will. A belief here and a practice there, religion *a la carte*.

False Belief 2

Some gurus claim secularisation has erased moral consciousness, so secular people are simply 'immoral'.

Not so. Secular people participate in many moral struggles and make an unprecedented number of moral choices. No longer 'programmed' by Christianity, they mostly get their morals from parents, peers and pop culture. The 20th century saw an explosion of moral causes – civil rights, human rights, women's rights, animal rights, pro-life, pro-choice, anti-nuclear, anti-apartheid. There were humanitarian movements for refugees, famine victims, prisoners of conscience, and endangered species. As Harold Turner said in an Asbury lecture: "Even the terrorist is driven by a moral passion."

False Belief 3

Some church leaders have a professor friend who has 'lost his faith' and so now they think every atheist is a philosophically sophisticated genius who has read every Christian book from Augustine to Zwingli and rejected the Christian case on rational grounds.

Not so. The vast majority of people are epistemologically unsophisticated. The 'thoughts' of many secular people are just reruns of popular ideas such as: "Too many hypocrites in the Church." The western mission field is filled with people who watch soap operas and believe life mirrors the tube. Most secular people have a religious agenda, and ask important religious questions (though not in traditional religious terms).

SECTION 3

JESUS THE EVANGELIST

"Great things happen when men and mountains meet, but these things do not happen when men jostle in the street."

– *William Blake*

"In a post-Christendom context, the Church is liberated from the corrupting influence of political, economic and social power. As a powerless minority of resident aliens in a culture that no longer accords Christianity special treatment, the Church is freed to live and witness in new ways. The Church is released from any sense of responsibility for supporting the *status quo*, or ensuring that history turns out the way it should. It can concentrate on simply being the Church, pointing towards a coming kingdom and, haltingly but with determination, embodying the values and ethos of that kingdom in its community life."

– *Stuart Murray*

book .link

Get a Grip on the Future
– Gerard Kelly, Word

Secularists, or people with no religious commitment, now form the second largest bloc in the world, second only to Christians and catching up fast.

Secularisation and the decline of Christendom has been bolstered by 6 key factors:

- **The Renaissance**, led by Erasmus and Bacon. The West rediscovered Greek philosophy, which pointed people away from God and back onto humanity. Suddenly the Christian world view was under attack, and seeds were planted for humanism.
- **The Reformation**, led by Luther and Calvin. The Church was turned away from its role in society in order to deal with its own internal divisions. It was said in Luther's time that 'Erasmus laid the egg, and Luther hatched it.'
- **Nationalism**, dividing Europe, destroying a sense of common humanity – and providing the basis for the two world wars of this century that caused so many to lose faith in God. Protestant Christianity didn't challenge nationalism: In some cases, it canonized nationalism.
- **The rise of science** challenged Christendom's pre-scientific ideas about the universe. The Church tried to silence science, forbidding Leonardo's studies of corpses, and forcing Galileo to disown his studies in astronomy.
- **The Enlightenment** built upon the Renaissance with its confidence in the power of human reason. With the Enlightenment came the appeal for human dignity and human rights. The Church opposed the Enlightenment – and something happens to the Church's credibility when she fails to throw her weight behind movements for justice and democracy.
- **Urbanisation** saw just 20 per cent of the US population settled in urban areas in 1870 – 90 per cent are in cities in 2000. Some would argue that the parish system does not provide proportionate per capita ministry for the cities. Others would say that an alienation from the natural revelation of the countryside contributes to a godless world view.

Britain – a postmodern culture

Change is here to stay, and it's proving hard to live with. People are facing isolation due to the breakdown of community, the pressures of urban life, the changes in gender roles, economic uncertainty and moral confusion. Dissatisfaction with life, even desperation, is mirrored in the explosion of interest in self-help and counselling, and a spiralling suicide rate. With these pressures there is a renewed

GOOD NEWS OR OLD NEWS?

A post-Christian society presents a very different mission context from a supposedly Christian or pre-Christian society. Lesslie Newbigin says our society is "a pagan society, and its paganism, having been born out of the rejection of Christianity, is far more resistant to the gospel than the pre-Christian paganism with which cross-cultural missions have been familiar."

In a pre-Christian society Christianity is news, presenting another religious and social option. There is a freshness and challenge about it that demands a response. In a post-Christian society it is difficult to persuade people that Christianity has anything fresh to offer. The assumption is that it has been tried and found wanting, and that wherever else answers to spiritual questions are to be found it is not in Christianity.

Evangelism in a post-Christian context is faced with the task not only of persuading people that Christianity is true but of even gaining a hearing for something widely regarded as *passé*.

A WINDOW ON POSTMODERNITY

"Postmodernity now exhibits scepticism about such 'grand narratives', towards the very idea that there are big systems of truth and explanation which will give us the key to understanding the world aright.

"Instead, the culture of consumption turns everything, including truth and knowledge themselves, into marketable consumer items. Citizens become consumers and goods themselves are valued not for their use, but for the meaning they bestow. People find significance in the very act of consumption to the extent that 'I shop, therefore I am' has become one of the slogans of postmodernity.

"It comes as no surprise, therefore, to read that loneliness is a sad and constant companion for many people. And yet the irony is that even this becomes exploited by the economism of our postmodern consumer culture, with no longer any attempt at subtlety. Lonely? You can buy or rent your own 'date' on video, especially selected just for you (and anyone else who pays) for viewing in a darkened room, with or without explicit sex. Wanting relationships? You can share intimate talk for hours on (highly profitable) telephone chat lines with people of similar sexual orientation, all available for just 49 pence a unit by ringing one of these numbers.

"The total price for such mass-produced, disembodied 'intimacy' is simply a video shop subscription, a large phone bill, and a greater emptiness than ever when you switch off the set or put the receiver down." – *Elaine Storkey*

interest in and respect for the spiritual dimensions of life. On the one hand, this represents an opportunity. On the other hand, this is the postmodern denial of objective truth that leaves the Church as merely one voice competing in a busy marketplace of ideas and beliefs.

book.link

Trend
– Sue Rinaldi, Word

So what specific challenges do we face in presenting the good news to post-Christian, postmodern Britain?

Our culture sees faith as a private matter

In a sacral society such as Europe under Christendom, religion permeates every aspect of society – politics, economics, social policy, the arts, legislation, etc. But secularism has now become the dominant philosophy in all areas of life, saving only the private sphere for spirituality.

As far as evangelism is concerned, there is freedom to proclaim the gospel but the temptation is strong to preach an anaemic privatised version that does not engage with contemporary issues.

"You show me your truth, and I'll show you mine."
– The Manic Street Preachers

Our culture sees faith as a commitment to 'a truth' rather than 'the truth'

In a sacral society there is little room for choice or diversity. Pluralisation means that there are many options on everything from washing powder to religion.

Pluralism goes further and argues that not only are there many options but each should be regarded as equally valid.

"In a postmodern environment evangelism will be much easier and discipleship much harder."
– Os Guinness

This presents Christianity, a religion with absolute truth claims, with a tricky situation. The endorsement of pluralism would dishonour Christ, but a society where choice can be freely exercised is an ideal environment for genuine faith to emerge. The challenge is to find ways of endorsing pluralisation and supporting religious freedom and the rights of minorities, whilst at the same time inviting people to choose to follow one who claimed to be the only way to God.

? Can we be equally passionate about calling people to follow Christ and defending their right to choose not to?

MORE ON POSTMODERNISM

Our society is experiencing a cultural shift that may be as significant as the last major cultural shift, which we know as the Enlightenment. That shift from the medieval to the modernist world view had huge ramifications for the churches and for evangelism, both positive and negative, but modernity is now under threat from postmodernity.

Central aspects of modernity are:

- reason is the basis for knowledge and decision-making.
- objectivity is possible because subject and object are separate.
- the world operates through the interplay of cause and effect.
- progress, development and modernisation are worthy and achievable goals: all problems are solvable.
- only scientifically established facts can be trusted; values are unreliable, matters of opinion only. Policies are to be based on facts.
- people are regarded as free and autonomous individuals.

Postmodernity represents a challenge to these beliefs. The main features of this include:

- the reliance on reason alone is regarded as reductionist and inadequate. Science does not have all the answers, nor is it equipped to deal with certain questions. The exclusion of other areas of human experience in making discoveries and decisions is unhelpful. The persistence of religion in atheistic societies is significant.
- keeping subject and object apart is regarded as impossible – there is interaction between them. Pure objectivity is a myth; presuppositions are involved. The result of this emphasis is a mechanistic approach to the world and exploitation of the environment.
- cause and effect is reductionist and excludes questions of meaning and purpose, which are important to everyone. We cannot live in a world that has no meaning.
- the optimism that all problems are solvable has been destroyed; the evolution of the human race towards maturity received a major setback in two world wars; development for part of the world has been attained through exploiting the rest of it; advances in technology have solved some problems but created others, and the destruction of the world through nuclear weapons or ecological disaster is a possible fruit of such progress.
- scientists operate with their own belief-systems.
- the emphasis on freedom and individualism has worked against community and social justice. Persons know themselves as persons in relationship.

(This portion derived and adapted from Graham Cray's booklet *From Here to Where?*)

The main tenets of postmodernity (apart from the above critique of modernism):

- a commitment to relativism in relation to questions of truth. There are no absolutes. Truth is in the mind of the believer as much as beauty is in the eye of the beholder.
- meaning is subjective rather than objective. When looking at a text, the original intention of the author is irrelevant: a text means whatever the reader understands by it (the "reader-response" theory in biblical criticism).
- spiritual values are significant and belief systems must be taken seriously, though without allowing claims to exclusivity. Imagination is necessary as well as rationality. Society is secular in the sense that no one value system will dominate, but not in the sense that spirituality will be downgraded.
- the world is seen through a biological rather than mechanistic model: concern for the environment and understanding of humanity as part of the environment rather than separate from it.
- institutions, hierarchies and structures are distrusted in favour of networks and grass-roots activities. Styles of organisation and leadership are changing. Male domination is challenged.
- iconoclasm – a refusal to give respect to established traditions or to take anything, including itself, too seriously. An emphasis on the chaotic and fragmentary rather than order and harmony. Readiness to hold together contradictory beliefs. Deep scepticism.
- pluralism – a commitment to choice at every level; a recognition that modern culture is diverse, global and a morass of constantly shifting subcultures; questions of truth are set within a context of pluralism.
- diversity – pick-and-mix society, collage, pastiche, rough edges, discord, merging the cultural and the commercial, the medium as the message, style rather than content, throw-away culture.

It is too early to say whether the shift will be complete or permanent, but there appear to be challenges and opportunities for evangelism.

In a postmodern culture spiritual issues are back on the agenda, but absolute truth claims are not. Unwarranted faith in technology, reason and materialism is being eroded, but pessimism and cynicism are growing. It has been suggested that in a postmodern environment evangelism will be much easier but discipleship much harder.

– *Stuart Murray*

SECTION 3

JESUS THE EVANGELIST

"Today there is almost a complete ignorance of what the Christian gospel really is. You see, Christian knowledge and awareness are now the echo of an echo of an echo – too faint to be heard. This means, for example, a feeling of awkwardness, even embarrassment, at entering a sacred building. There is ignorance in the ways of Christian worship. Therefore such people no longer desire to enter churches. It means an almost complete ignorance of Christian stories, biblical references, or the traditional language of the pulpit."

– Alan Walker

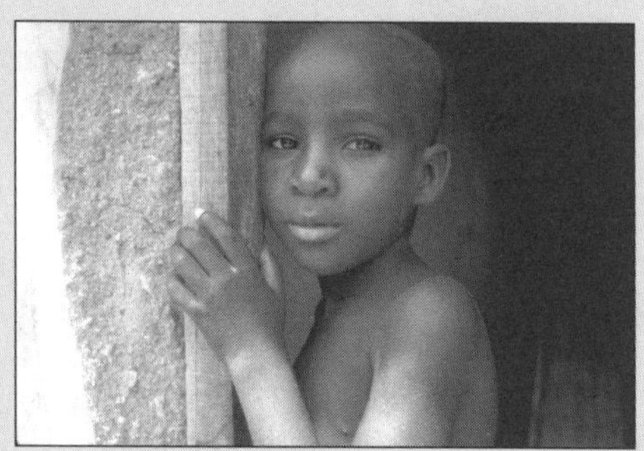

"If we see the gospel message primarily in terms of being saved from our sins, we have a significant evangelistic problem in that our increasingly post-Christendom and postmodern society has a very poor awareness of its sinfulness. We're in danger of preaching a solution to people who don't even acknowledge that the problem really exists. It's not surprising that for many people our message seems to be of limited relevance."

– Chris Thackery

Our culture is largely ignorant about the Christian faith

In a post-Christian society, the central facts of the Christian story are not well known and it is vital not to assume otherwise. Recent research has shown that those under 40 have only a sketchy knowledge of the life of Jesus or the biblical narrative – and often what they do know is inaccurate. Evangelism will not be able to operate any longer under the assumption that its task is to call people to a deeper commitment to a story they already know.

Our culture is not strongly conscious of guilt

The assumption has been that everyone is aware of sin and guilt and that it is good news to discover that God is willing to forgive sins and remove guilt. Although this is in fact only one gospel motif among many others, it has been predominant and remains so in contemporary evangelism.

But it seems that post-Christendom is not a 'guilt culture'. A very large number of people in our society do not feel guilty. Recent research in the UK indicates that nearly half of those interviewed who had recently become Christians did not respond because they felt guilty. They responded to Jesus Christ for other reasons.

Issues of sin and guilt were confronted at a later stage, but these were not what attracted them to Christianity. Evangelists in this context appear to have two options: to try to make people feel guilty in order to offer them freedom from guilt, or to recover other dimensions of the gospel that connect with contemporary felt needs.

Our culture does not value churchgoing

Much evangelism depends upon people coming to church buildings or church events. It is as if we have read the word 'go' in the Great Commission but heard 'come'. In post-Christian Europe and North America where going to church is no longer natural or congenial, evangelism that relies on a 'come' methodology is going to be ineffective.

The phrase 'new evangelism' is being used increasingly in the UK. It has five key characteristics; it is relational, contextual, humble, patient and holistic. Not everyone will be happy with this shift, and it is not without its dangers, but we are unlikely to see a widespread return to evangelistic practices that rely heavily on dogmatic proclamation, mass events and cold contact with strangers.

JESUS IS MY PERSONAL SAVIOUR

There is no God-framework in society. In a secular society, religion is permitted access to only the private sphere of values and leisure interests. Any attempts to apply the gospel to business ethics, international affairs or housing policies will be regarded as intrusion – unless these attempts are seen as buttressing the *status quo*.

If the Church under Christendom played a priestly role, under secularism it is confined to a monastic role: its true prophetic role is welcome in neither context. As far as social action is concerned, there is a temptation to restrict our activities to this private sphere, to care for the casualties of society rather than challenging the unjust structures that result in casualties.

JESUS IS THE ANSWER – BUT WHAT IS THE QUESTION?

Christendom was a 'guilt culture', but not all societies are. Some African societies are fear cultures. Japan has been described as a shame culture.

This means that evangelists need to listen carefully to the culture in which they are working. What questions are being asked? What issues are important? What are the felt needs? What biblical themes are relevant? Where are the contact points? What can be affirmed in the culture? What needs to be challenged? If Jesus is the answer, what is the question? Our search is not for a comfortable or acceptable message but for a challenging and appropriate one.

It is important to recognise the variety of themes in the New Testament – a very broad spectrum, many messages, focal points and applications, rich resources rather than a narrow message. We can see the New Testament itself as an example of contextualising the message from a Jewish to a Gentile audience (e.g. justification as law court image, redemption as slave market image, *logos* as philosophical concept).

There are many other possible starting points apart from guilt, such as shame, loneliness, suffering, injustice, insecurity, insignificance.

TOO BUSY TO EVANGELISE?

In a postmodern culture, where institutions are suspect and commitment to such institutions is waning, churches will need to think carefully about how they operate. The Church remains crucial to evangelism, but only as it rediscovers its calling to be a missionary community, a 'Church for others', will it be the good news it wants to share.

Churches that want to evangelise their communities will concentrate on equipping their members for life in society rather than using up all their free time in church activities.

Our Message

Just exactly what is the good news of Jesus that we want to proclaim?

What is our message for the sinned-against? For the happy pagan? For the moral crusader? There is a need for many different evangelistic messages, prophetic evangelism, contextual evangelism. There is a need for more than just illustrations – presenting the heart of the gospel in many ways. There is a need for careful listening and reflection.

This last summer, the following 'evangelistic' signboards were displayed outside churches in Tulsa, Oklahoma:

- 'Eternity – smoking or non-smoking?'
- 'Come in and have a faith lift.'
- 'If you think it's hot here, just wait.' (*During a heatwave in which numbers of people died.*)

Are these accurate representations of the message of Jesus?

Questioning our message 1

"It's all about heaven and hell" – Jesus for the future

Death and Hell – Evangelical Alliance, Paternoster

"After attending a number of evangelism training courses," Walter Fahrer writes, "I can give you the classic elements of an evangelical gospel presentation:

- God is holy.
- people are sinful.
- a gulf separates people from God.
- the cross of Jesus is a bridge that brings God and people together.
- believing in Jesus is the ticket to heaven.

But what about:

- Discipleship and relationship now?
- Life before death?
- The church as 'a waiting room for the second coming'?"

Many Christians can describe the four steps that we need to take to be saved from our sins and born again. Considerably fewer can talk

EXTRA ORDINARY EVANGELISTS

Manchester is witnessing some remarkable changes – rapid city living expansion projects, an increasingly cosmopolitan culture, a growing importance on the national and international stage. But the transformation on the spiritual landscape is perhaps even more impressive.

Many believe the two are linked.

A dynamic prayer network among churches of many streams and denominations is the backdrop for rapidly growing and increasingly effective youth ministries. Planet Life, a youth worship night in the city's leading rock venue, draws monthly crowds of 2,500. Among the brave new incarnational youthwork strategies an important example is Eden. And lined up for this summer, to raise the temperature even higher, is Soul Survivor: The Message 2000 – a full on urban adventure with its finger firmly on the nation's pulse.

Never far away from the action, in fact often at the centre of it, you'll find young women and men from The Message, a ministry founded in 1992 by Andy Hawthorne. This community of evangelists share a dream to engage with, and bring transformation to, the world around them.

Sixty Eden team members have been picked by The Message and positioned in two of Manchester's toughest spots – Wythenshawe and Salford. As people they're quite ordinary to look at. They come from pretty ordinary families. They have ordinary jobs and ordinary houses. But they follow the example of Jesus. If you were to meet one they'd probably get quite excited about the fact that Jesus found himself 12 ordinary mates and spent three years meeting ordinary people.

God's heart is to restore his relationship with the people he created. He didn't send a fax to earth, he sent his son. Eden follows that example. Most team members have discarded comfy suburban homes, even promising careers and precious relationships, to live among and reach out to ordinary people in Manchester. To the community around them who've never heard the gospel they become the gospel. You could describe their technique as 'word become flesh'. All the signs herald an end to old fashioned 'hit and run' evangelism and the dawn of a new era of disciple making. Tens of young people are reached every week and at last churches in these tough areas are starting to grow – spiritually and numerically. The Message firmly believe now is the time to roll out the Eden project all over the toughest parts of Manchester.

Soul Survivor has borrowed this evangelistic paradigm for its summer event Soul Survivor: The Message 2000 and is magnifying it on a vast scale. The organisers expect the challenging nature of the event to generate 20,000 extra ordinary evangelists who will demonstrate the life and love of Jesus to a city desperate to know it.

Street Invaders and Urban Exposure summer teams have reached into similar hard-to-crack communities. Like Eden they know that it simply is not good enough to talk the message – you have to be the message.

ENDLESS BLISS AND PINK CANDY FLOSS CLOUDS

Eternal life is never presented in the New Testament simply as a forever existence of bliss, no work, and harp playing. Eternal life is more that quantitive but qualitative – because it is a life with the Jesus who has beaten death. We are able to conquer the power of death because we are with him and in him.

anything like so clearly about what we're saved for, still less how to do it.

We see so many Christians whose early growth has reached a plateau, whose new life has calcified into routine. Although few would admit it rationally, there's an underlying thought that if I'm saved and going to heaven, what need is there for anything else? Where there's no real vision of the purpose of discipleship, living out New Testament principles can quickly decay into a legalistic chore. Even where people have a vision to grow, our theology of discipleship usually fails to give the practical tools that are necessary to pursue it.

Questioning our message 2

"It's all about forgiveness of sins" – Jesus for the past

The Western church has for centuries regarded the cross as the centrepiece of Christian doctrine, and seen salvation primarily in terms of the forgiveness of sins. This is so familiar to us that it comes as something of a surprise to find that the early Christians had a different perspective. The early Christians certainly preached the cross, but they equally emphasised the resurrection: "Christ is risen" was their glorious news. It was their proof that the life that Jesus himself had and the life to the full he promised to his followers was real, and was powerful enough to conquer death.

Questioning our message 3

"It's all about people realising they can't live life to the full without knowing Jesus" – Jesus as a self-improvement programme

Another problem is that presenting the gospel so heavily weighted towards the forgiveness of sins creates a gravitational pull towards a human-centred perspective. God's primary purpose becomes the rescue of humanity from the Fall. Self-centeredness is, of course, a disease endemic to sinful man, but sadly our theology has proved too accommodating. We have churches full of people who respond to God as though his primary purpose is to solve their problems, make them feel better, and who continue to live in the I-centred world of their old nature.

Our message – some of the above – and yet much more

We need to take a fresh look at what we understand by the gospel. We need to add a far greater emphasis on what we're saved for, on

JESUS FOR THE PAST

If we look at Jesus' own teaching then certainly we see the themes of repentance, reconciliation and ransom woven throughout. But we also see that in fact a greater proportion of his teaching focuses on kingdom, and on true life. The coming kingdom is a repeated theme, and a large number of his parables communicate the nature of this kingdom and how to enter it. He taught about the necessity for newness of life; his Sermon on the Mount describes how this life is to be lived, and central to his message is the declaration that in him is abundant life: '"I have come that they may have life, and have it to the full"' (John 10:10). It's a life of true freedom, a life that is so powerful that it gushes like streams from within, empowers us to reign over our present circumstances and lasts for eternity.

The preoccupation of the Western church with salvation in terms of forgiveness of sins emerged some centuries later. It was at a time when much of the life spark of the early Christians had dimmed, when the Church had transformed from a radical persecuted sect into the official religion of the Roman Empire. It's interesting to note in passing that even the use of the cross as a symbol in Christian art didn't emerge until well into the fifth century.

THE LOST

Some suggest that it is demeaning and inappropriate to view those outside of Christ as 'lost.' Bearing in mind Jesus' clear claims to be 'The Way' in John's gospel and his three pictures of lostness – sheep, coin and son – in Luke 15, it is hard to support that conclusion.

If a person is to become 'found,' there must be a willingness to admit that they have lost their way – otherwise Jesus becomes just another one of many signposts alongs a vague spiritual journey.

JESUS THE REAL LIFE

Preaching that is Fall/Redemption centred tends to start off with human need – the idea is that we have a problem, and God moves in to fix it for us. But we need to declare a message where Jesus is the first and last – the beginning and the end – so we must declare a Creation/Fall/Redemption message:

- good news first – God is the author and creator of life
- bad news next – the Fall is man's rebellion to God's purposes
- more good news – God initiates again by sending Jesus to be our redeemer and rescuer.

Humanity's response to God's first great work – Creation – was an act of wilful rebellion. So what will our response be to God's second great work – redemption through Christ?

"In the spiritual renaissance that I believe is coming to birth, it will not be the message of Paul that this time galvanizes hearts, as in the Reformation and the Wesleyan revival, but the human figure of Jesus."
– *Walter Wink*

Engaging the Powers
– Walter Wink, Mowbray

"God blessed them and said to them, 'Be fruitful and increase in number; fill the earth and subdue it. Rule over the fish of the sea and the birds of the air and over every living creature that moves on the ground.' "
– *Genesis 1:28*

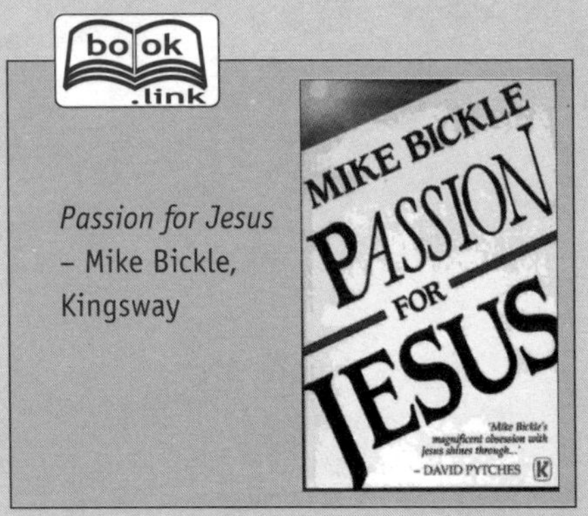

Passion for Jesus
– Mike Bickle, Kingsway

abundant life and on discipleship. We would not want in any way to undermine the cosmic significance of the cross, or the profound importance of the forgiveness of sins, and reconciliation to our Father in heaven. But the gospel as portrayed in the Bible is bigger than the one we have been preaching. We need to add these dimensions to our message, presenting a more faithful, relevant, attractive, and contagious gospel. What does this message look like?

Jesus the centre again

It may seem obvious that the good news is about Jesus, but we need to reaffirm that the gospel is centred in a person rather than a set of propositions about a person. Jesus is attractive to people.

- **Jesus the real life**. Our gospel message must begin not with mankind, or with the Fall, but with God himself, and with his purposes even before the creation of the world.

God gave Adam and Eve the breathtaking privilege of being involved in his plans to fill the earth with his family. He also called them to rule the earth – giving them, like himself, a purpose, and authority under his own authority. This is the glorious life we were designed for; joyous intimacy with God, purpose, and a connection to the mains power supply: drawing life and the power to live directly from the source himself.

- **Jesus the eternal life**. The book of Revelation shows us where God's plans lead: we see our destination there. We shall see him face to face. We shall reign with him, celebrate with him, glorify him and be glorified by him. We shall be full of eternal life, living in a city which shines with the glory of God, where there is perfect peace, fulfilment, excitement, truth, justice, plenty of all we need, laughter, a wedding feast, the never-ending banquet.
- **Jesus the way**. Human beings, cut off from the mains supply of life, are running on batteries. These run out at death. Some people are trying to get back to God through philosophy, good deeds and religion: to no avail.

But what humanity cannot do, God did. Jesus came into the world bringing a message of hope: new birth to a new life, life to the full, living in the kingdom of God. Jesus is the bridge from death to life.

- Once over the bridge, our new life has just begun. Our purpose is to glorify God in everything we do. But we have been dam-

EVANGELISM BEYOND THE FRINGE

There is a way to reach today's postmodern and post-Christian generation – argues Joseph Steinberg, co-creator of The Y Course.

Today's 'unbelievers' are quite unlike those of ten years ago. Which is the reason the new and acclaimed evangelistic course – The Y Course – was created.

The content speaks powerfully to people who – at best – see the Church and Christianity as no more exciting than chewing cardboard. It explores life rather than religion, tells the story of Jesus rather than covering issues about discipleship, faces the questions people really are genuinely concerned about, and gives people ample time to process what they discover.

The approach of the course – and its content – has much to say about the kind of evangelism needed to make an impact in our post-Christian and postmodern world.

Great message – wrong audience

First there's the need to match the message with the audience. Steinberg calls it "The Peter-Paul Dissonance." Peter's Day of Pentecost message in Jerusalem was vastly different to Paul's in Athens. Both urged their audience to repentance and faith – yet their content and approach were poles apart.

Peter quoted from Scriptures his hearers knew and trusted, pointed to the impact Jesus had made among them – and saw instant results. In contrast, Paul pointed his audience to the natural creation, quoted from their secular poets for support – and gave them time to process what they heard.

The stark difference is because Peter spoke to God-fearing Jewish minds steeped in the knowledge of God's dealings with his people. And Paul addressed superstitious Gentiles who had questions about life but to whom God was unknown.

The lesson screams out. God calls us to shape our message to the mind-set, culture and felt needs of our audience.

We are not to present the equivalent of Peter's Jerusalem message – designed for God-fearing, Bible-knowing people – to an audience has no background in the Bible, no knowledge of the story of Jesus and no understanding as to what a Christian is.

Paul's message in Athens – recorded in Acts 17:22-31 – has much to say about the content of our message today. He started where his listeners were – with what they already accepted as true. He moved on to explain the true nature and character of God – a God who is greater than all he created.

To support his claims Paul quoted from the culture of his hearers , speaking of their need to have a totally different view about God. He went on to warn them of a coming judgement which would be just and fair – while announcing the way to pass through that judgement justly.

Paul also spoke of the resurrection as the ultimate proof that what he said was true. And every word he used was well within the understanding of his hearers. We should do exactly the same. Indeed, this is exactly the way The Y Course does it.

Responding to the po-mo culture

Taking today's audience seriously also means facing up to another profound cultural change – labelled 'postmodernity'. Truth has become an individual matter. For the po-mo (postmodern) mind, the only real truth is there is no truth – only experience. There is no a big picture of history that makes sense; no reason for life to have meaning or purpose.

At the same time, po-mo culture believes each person's story and experience is valid and deserves to be heard. It has a very real openness to spirituality – particularly when it has nothing to do with institutional structures. Which is why crystals and such like are cool and the church is crass.

That is the territory The Y Course charts. It avoids quoting people as authorities, or arguing from the abstract concepts of the Epistles. It's crammed with stories. Incidents in the life of Jesus, the first garden and its demise through human sinfulness, the lost son and even Little Red Riding Hood.

Red socks and wedding vows

However, the right approach and the right content have to be embedded in effective communication. In particular, that means steering clear of the abstract concepts that make communication so hard in our visually concrete age.

So The Y Course avoids the approach of the Epistles – written to help the followers of Jesus do better. Instead it draws almost entirely on the Gospels, and lets the story of Jesus and the stories he told speak powerfully for themselves.

The Y Course also includes a host of fresh and compelling illustrations. For example, there's the comparison between salvation by grace or works - conveyed through the reward vouchers saved up from a local grocery store, with the recording angel explaining, 'Sorry you're four vouchers short.'

There's the impact that just one red sock makes in a load of white laundry and just the merest smear of soap in a glass of water to convey why God doesn't lower the pass mark and let a few sinful people into his heaven.

Joseph Steinberg, a seasoned missionary and local church leader created The Y Course in partnership with communications specialist Peter Meadows and Agape staff members Roger and Donna Vann. This article is adapted from Renewal magazine June 1999.

"For whoever wants to save his life will lose it, but whoever loses his life for me will save it."

– Luke 9:24

"Jesus looked at him and loved him. 'One thing you lack,' he said. 'Go, sell everything you have and give to the poor, and you will have treasure in heaven. Then come, follow me.' "

– Mark 10:21

"If any man builds on this foundation using gold, silver, costly stones, wood, hay or straw, his work will be shown for what it is, because the Day will bring it to light. It will be revealed with fire, and the fire will test the quality of each man's work. If what he has built survives, he will receive his reward. If it is burned up, he will suffer loss; he himself will be saved, but only as one escaping through the flames."

– 1 Cor 3:12–15

The Nazareth Manifesto
"The Spirit of the Lord is on me, because he has anointed me to preach good news to the poor. He has sent me to proclaim freedom for the prisoners and recovery of sight for the blind, to release the oppressed, to proclaim the year of the Lord's favour."

– Luke 4:18,19

aged and scarred by our experiences in a fallen world. To realise the fullness of life given to us, we work together with God to nurture the growth of our new life up to full stature.

This is the process of discipleship: working with God to be transformed into his likeness. We truly live when we truly love; we truly love when we sacrifice.

Jesus – the one we follow always

As disciples, we have a new identity. As people of the kingdom of God, living according to the will of God, our every action has awesome new potential. Jesus says that godly deeds store up treasure in heaven.

Paul explains to the Corinthians that all our works will be tested, and that which is built of gold will endure.

As disciples we are dealing every moment with choices that have an eternal dimension.

Jesus – good news for the poor

The kingdom of God is an upside-down kingdom. The model of Jesus shows us that grass-roots action is more significant than trying to influence the movers and shakers of society. Jesus chose to be identified with the poor, the weak, the marginalised, those without voices or status. He adopted as his agenda for mission the Nazareth Manifesto (Luke 4:18, 19).

What might this mean? Holistic mission, which refuses to separate social justice from evangelism? Decades of Justice as well as Decades of Evangelism? Church planters prioritising poor communities as they decide where to plant churches? Evangelists discovering how to bring good news to the 'sinned against' as well as to sinners? Pastors empowering the weaker and less articulate members of their churches? Churches becoming communities of liberation and hope?

Considering our method

Learning from the Jesus model

The culture Jesus operated in

To better understand the radical nature of Jesus the evangelist, we first need to understand the culture and context into which he came. When Jesus began his public ministry on earth around AD 26 in the Palestinian backwaters of the Roman Empire, there were four main

JUBILEE

The 'year of the Lord's favour' is thought by many scholars to be a reference to the neglected 'year of Jubilee', the foundation of Old Testament economic legislation in Leviticus 25.

Was Jesus announcing that it was time to practise Jubilee? His disciples were initially appalled at the implications, but it is arguable that the economic life of the Jerusalem church, described in Acts 4–5, was a determined attempt to contextualise the Jubilee provisions. A national Jubilee was not feasible, but within this growing church radical steps could be taken to remove the extremes of wealth and poverty and to share resources.

The result – "There were no needy persons among them" (Acts 4:34) – certainly represents the aim of the Jubilee legislation. Post-Christendom churches, responding to the challenge to be good news to the poor, may explore creative ways of practising Jubilee. Inspired by the Nazareth Manifesto, churches in a post-Christendom society may no longer be alienated from the poor, but communities of good news to the poor.

GOOD WORKS

The Celtic saints are well-known for their devout spirituality and energetic missionary zeal, yet the monasteries they founded gave daily food to the poor and men like Cuthbert habitually spent themselves on the needy.

John Wesley, motivated by a passion for making disciples, found it necessary to address social injustice as he preached to the marginalised. Converts from the mines and the industrializing north of England found themselves arguing for justice and leading the newly born trade-union movement.

William Booth, founder of the Salvation Army, found his destiny amongst the poor in London's East End. Preaching the gospel and winning converts, he soon realised that attendance at meetings was not sufficient to enable effective discipleship. Hence he set about creating employment to fill the hours of the day which might otherwise be dedicated to drinking. Match factories were opened and the first labour exchange in London was started, pre-empting government action by 30 years. In September 1890 Booth published *In Darkest England and the Way Out*, an early attempt to apply the Christian ethic to industrial civilisation.

The historian Kathleen Heasman has estimated that in the second half of the 19th century in Britain 'three-quarters of the total number of voluntary charitable foundations may be regarded as evangelical in character and control.' They included:

- Ragged Schools, providing education, food, clothing and training for poor children.
- Orphanages started by George Muller, Charles Spurgeon and Dr Barnardo.
- The Young Men's Christian Association (YMCA) with close links to D.L. Moody.
- The Temperance Movement of local groups operating in the 1820s and two national societies set up in the 1850s.
- The work of Ellice Hopkins with prostitutes and provision of education for their children (societies for 'friendless girls').
- Medical missions.
- Prison Gate Missions – prison visiting and an early form of probation work.

"Gimmicks, pseudo-questionnaires, buttonholing, evangelical mugging, and the outright rudeness of some witnesses offend the sensitivities of caring Christians. The end result is that evangelism becomes a much misunderstood term, one which people either swear by ... or at."

– Dr. Joseph C. Aldrich

Man to Man: Friendship and Faith
– Steven Croft, Scripture Union

Lifestyle Evangelism
– Joe Aldrich, Multnomah Press

religious groups with which he had to contend and contrast his ministry.

These four groups were united in a common aim – bringing the kingdom of God on earth. However, if their aim united them, their methods divided them.

The Jews had been oppressed for 300 years when Jesus came – first by the Greeks and then by the Romans. Their expectations concerning the nature of the Messiah and how he would spread the good news of the kingdom of God were both high and somewhat fixed in the direction of military intervention. If Jesus were to fit his message and his method into the existing social context, then he had four possible options available.

How Jesus didn't share his message

- **Compromise** – The Messiah with a smile and a handshake: the Sadducees.

The Sadducees were a group of Jews who had emerged as Israel's chief negotiators with the Romans. They were despised as a compromised people.

- **Legalism** – The Messiah with a frown and a law book: the Pharisees.

Manoeuvring for political compromise under the leadership of Judas Maccabeus had badly damaged their cause and power base. By Jesus' time the Pharisees had hypocritically reached a position of enjoying the advantages gained by the negotiations of the Sadducees, whilst at the same time warning against them.

- **Violence and coercion** – The Messiah with an Uzi: the Zealots

In the face of considerable oppression from the Romans, these Jews believed that God wanted his chosen people to be free and that the end would justify the means, to the point where violence was not only permissible but desirable.

- **Separation from the big, bad world** – The Messiah as monk in the wilderness: the Essenes

It was the Essenes who left us the legacy of the Qumran Texts (Dead Sea Scrolls). John the Baptist may well have had an Essene upbring-

THE SADDUCEES

Despised as political compromisers, the Sadducees achieved some very useful bargains for the Jews.

For example, the Jews in all Roman conquered nations did not have to provide male slaves to the Roman army, and they didn't have to indulge in emperor worship.

The Sadducees had ingratiated themselves well with the Romans; not least by levying various temple taxes, and using the money thus raised to lend to the Roman administration and to the Roman army. The Sadducees base their theological perspective on the Pentateuch and consequently had little understanding of physical resurrection, the existence of angels or indeed of an after-life.

THE PHARISEES

Although pledged to poverty and not officially allowed to accrue wealth themselves, the Pharisees wielded an awesome amount of power amongst the Jews as the primary interpreters of the law and consequently attracted large amounts of personal sponsorship as they wandered, heavily disliked, amongst the ordinary Jews dressed, as they were, in their white robes. An outward observance of the law, politics and religion hid inward corruption and it was the Pharisees who came in for the heaviest criticism from Jesus for those very reasons (see Matt 23).

THE ZEALOTS

The Zealots believed that God was pleased with those Zealots who killed the most Romans, a Jewish form of *jihad*. The Zealots were violent activists who looked to force of arms to wrest power and political control from the privileged Romans and give it back to the oppressed Jews. Many Jews whilst not being Zealots believed that the awaited Messiah would be a warrior king, who would do just that. Interestingly Simon, one of Jesus' disciples, is described as a Zealot (Luke 6:15).

THE ESSENES

The Essenes judged the Sadducees to be compromisers, the Pharisees to be corrupt and the Zealots to be violent; and so they sought a place in the wilderness where they could build a good and perfect community and serve God's people Israel spiritually (hence the accuracy and preservation of the Dead Sea Scrolls by an Essene community at Qumran). Not only were the Essenes not of the world, they were hardly even in it.

ing, as reflected in his style of ministry – seclusion and somewhat peculiar separatism.

These were the four major expectations for Jesus, and the context and culture in which he began his evangelism. But Jesus rejected all four as his message or method of spreading the good news of the kingdom of God. The way of Jesus the evangelist was radical, and yet managed to fulfil the four major signs the Jews anticipated as the authentication of the Messiah who was to come.

"Kingdom people seek first the kingdom of God and its justice; church people often put church work above concerns for justice, mercy and truth. Church people think about how to get people into the Church; kingdom people think about how to get the Church into the world. Church people worry that the world might change the Church; kingdom people work to see the Church change the world."

– Howard Snyder

? Have we (the modern Church) embraced the methods Jesus chose not to use?

Signs of the kingdom

The Jews of Jesus' time always wanted to see this kingdom and were looking out for certain hallmarks of the kingdom.

They were:

- The presence of God among his people.
- The overthrow of the power of Satan.
- An outbreak of salvation.
- A new community of faith.

book.link

The Church Beyond the Congregation – James Thwaites, Paternoster

So the background context in which Jesus the evangelist operated gave him four options; and he pursued a fifth. The Jewish cultural background into which Jesus the evangelist operated looked for four signs of authentication of the coming kingdom of God; and Jesus fulfilled them all. The question remains: How did he do this?

The Jesus method of evangelism was based around incarnation and identification. This fifth option of Jesus the evangelist fulfilled the four signs of God's kingdom.

"The Word became flesh and made his dwelling among us."

– John 1:14

Jesus: incarnation rather than ghettoism

It is not enough for us to share information about Jesus. We must realize that the gospel is incarnational – it's about turning words into action in our own lives.

Literature distribution, Christian television and radio may have some limited effect, but the Jesus model demands that the message is *lived out* incarnationally by millions of people like us.

THE WORD

John's gospel was written in Greek, and the term which is translated into English as 'word' is *logos*. To the ancient Greek philosophers the *logos* was the ground of all being. To them it symbolised thought, ideas, and all that was best in everything. John took the idea of the *logos* and gave it a whole new meaning. In effect he was saying, 'You may think that the Word is a great idea, but I'm telling you that God's greatest idea, God's greatest thought and plan was Jesus. Jesus Christ is the *logos*.' By referring to the Word, John is speaking not only to the Greeks, but also to the Jews. How did God create the world? Genesis Chapter 1 tells us he did it by speaking. God said, 'Let there be light, and there was light' ... And God said, 'Let there be an expanse between the waters to separate water from water' ... And God said, 'Let dry ground appear. '... Then God said, 'Let the land produce vegetation ... ' and so on. God made things happen with a word. God spoke the universe into being. If he had remained silent nothing would have happened. So the Word is evident back in Genesis 1. John is saying that the Word, God's self-expression, is not only to be seen in the creation of the universe: the greatest expression of God is Jesus Christ.

GET DOWN SATAN

The Jews under Rabbinical law and at the time of Jesus also expected to recognise the kingdom of God by its defeat of Satan. This is why Jesus both taught and demonstrated that defeat (Acts 1:1) and why Jesus' evangelism was authenticated by many recorded episodes of healing and deliverance (14 such occurrences are recorded in Mark's gospel alone).

John recalls that Jesus came to defeat the works of the evil one (1 John 3:8). The cross was about such victory (Col 2:15) and the Early Church had to hijack a Greek word in order to explain this good news. That word *euangelion,* from which we get the word evangelism, was a military term meaning the proclamation or heralding of the military defeat of an enemy, freedom from oppression, safety and security, salvation, etc.

GOD WITH US

The Jews knew that when the kingdom of God broke out God would be present, real and immediate again, back with his people as he had been in the Old Testament.

For 400 to 500 years there had been a virtual silence from God between Old and New Testaments, but when the kingdom came (as John the Baptist prophesied it would) then the God who was everywhere would become again the Emmanuel, the God who is somewhere, living now in them by his Holy Spirit, and not just coming on them as his Holy Spirit did in the Old Testament. This sense of the presence of God the Old Testament calls *shekinah* (Glory of God), which means literally the 'weight of his presence', has always been a hallmark of the immediacy of the kingdom.

This presence of God has been a hallmark of every revival throughout Church history. In 1904, Welsh miners would literally fall before God's presence in the streets as they passed the chapels, and a judge in court would do the same before the testimony of a converted prisoner. In 1906 in the Azusa Street Revival in the USA the presence of God could be felt a quarter of a mile away from the revival meetings. American evangelist Charles Finney carried the kingdom of God and God's presence within him to such an extent that people in the street would rush up to him and fall at his feet in repentance. British evangelist Smith Wigglesworth would mount a train and have entire carriages coming to Christ simply because of the presence of God.

SECTION 3
JESUS THE EVANGELIST

Beyond the Fringe – Nick Pollard, IVP

"God's intention is that every congregation of believers in Jesus be a surprising revelation of the presence of the kingdom of God on earth. These surprising colonies of heaven are audiovisual expressions of the continuing life and ministry of Jesus in his fullness in an evil world."

– Shenk & Stutzman

Sowing, Reaping, Keeping – Laurence Singlehurst, Crossway Books

"Churches that become ghettoised and cut off from their communities tend to measure the commitment of their members by how many church services they attend – services and meetings, where, ironically, they discuss evangelism and pray for the very world that they have cut themselves off from."

The disclaimer 'don't look at the Church, look at Jesus' is theologically bankrupt. God wants our individual and corporate lives to be working models, walking demonstrations of the work and love of Jesus.

Incarnation 1: Being with 'sinners'

Jesus was a people person. He was the kind of person you would have on your dinner guest list.

Children loved him and had access to him (Mark 10:13–16). He related wonderfully to people at all levels – from one individual alone to thousands in a crowd.

He was open with his emotions, being frequently moved by compassion, anger and tears. He cried at the tomb of his friend, Lazarus (John 11:35), was moved to anger as he overlooked Jerusalem (Matt 23:37), and had compassion over the crowds (Matt 9:36).

This compassion often caused Jesus to take initiative (Luke 7:11–17). It frequently meant identification with the physically or ritually unclean (dead bodies, lepers, women in menstruation, people living amongst tombs). He deliberately touched people, even though touch wasn't necessary for him to heal people (Mark 1:40–45). The point of touch was surely more to do with identification, compassion, and affirmation.

One of his derogatory nicknames was 'friend of sinners'. He was fun, emotionally open, compassionate, patient, practically orientated, perceptive, passionate, provocative, a servant, a good questioner and yet directive. Lavish and personal in his praise of others, he was relevant and realistic in his illustrations and stories, emphatic in placing friendship before function, and generous with his time, food, and money.

Of the three years of his public ministry, some people estimate Jesus spent up to 50 per cent of his time with individuals; mainly in evangelism. Given that in this period Jesus had to reveal and explain the coming kingdom of God, establish himself as the Messiah of God and birth the Church, this is a staggering statistic.

SALVATION

The Jews anticipated that with the coming of the kingdom of God and its inherent good news would come an outbreak of salvation. In the Old Testament this has been foreshadowed by Jubilee, a time when all debts were cancelled, land redistributed, and slave set free as detailed in Isaiah 61. This anticipated salvation would be the equivalent of the Old Testament word *shalom*, used commonly as a greeting or blessing and meaning peace with God, peace with yourself and peace with one another. Its nearest equivalent in the New Testament lies in the Greek word *soteria*, which is interchangeably translated as salvation, wholeness, healing and forgiveness. Jesus the evangelist clearly links his gospel of the kingdom of God with this salvation in Luke 4, where he quotes from Isaiah and the Jubilee passages.

THE JESUS FAMILY

The Jews realised that the outbreak of God's kingdom as heralded by his Messiah would not only mean personal salvation, but would also create a faith community or a kingdom people, who would be citizens of a new order where the rule and reign of God was evident on earth. Corporate and not just individual salvation was to be a hallmark of God's kingdom, just as it would be a hallmark of Jesus the evangelist's ministry. This is in part why Jesus worked in a team. Jesus' teams were a demonstration of the creation of kingdom communities.

Jesus teamed up at a variety of levels. Jesus and John, the disciple whom he loved. Jesus and the triumvirate of Peter, James and John. There was Jesus and the twelve, Jesus and the seventy (or 72), Jesus and the 120. Post-resurrection: Jesus and the 500.

Jesus the Evangelist's view of corporate salvation is evidenced in his prayer for the believers in John 17. Eph 2:11–18 also describes our salvation in terms of reconciliation between Jesus and Gentiles.

The earthly ministry of Jesus the evangelist clearly demonstrated attempts to break down divisions between people groups and took his Jewish followers considerably by surprise, as their understanding of the kingdom people created by the Messiah of God did not include Gentiles.

THE WONDER OF INCARNATION

The incarnation is more than a wondrous theological truth – it is an example for us in our mission to make God known. The Jesus model is as follows: "As you sent me into the world, I have sent them into the world" – John 17:18.

Jesus the evangelist seems to have deliberately looked for ways in which he could identify with his listeners. The Church ever since seems to have been looking for ways in which they could be distinct from them.

We have to learn to live evangelistically in the real world rather than just do evangelism occasionally. That is not to say that there will not be times of coordinated outreach, special projects and missions. But the challenge that is inescapable is that, if we are to be like Jesus, we need to live as agents of the kingdom of God everywhere – all the time.

SECTION 3

JESUS THE EVANGELIST

"What is life, if we have not life together?"

– G K Chesterton

**"Sometimes you wanna go where everybody knows your name
And they're always glad you came
You wanna be where you can see
Troubles are all the same
You wanna go where everyone knows your name."**

– theme from Cheers

The Search for Intimacy
– Elaine Storkey, Hodder and Stoughton

> **Do you think that the evangelistic strategy of your church is weighted towards a 'come and hear' or towards a 'go and tell' approach? Do you have non–Christian friends with whom you spend quality social time? Could you be described as a 'friend of sinners?'**

Incarnation 2: Boldness required

Jesus did not hide in the cloisters of the temple, but went out to where sinful people were and took some serious risks – which many misunderstood. If we determine to take incarnational living seriously, it will change way we use our time and our homes, and the way we spend our money – it will also open us to accusations of compromise by religious people.

> **Where are the 'altars to the unknown gods' in your community? Can you use them to declare the gospel? How?**

Incarnation 3: Life together

Jesus called his disciples to a three-year adventure of life together, of laughter and tears, of breakthrough and frustration, of shared resources and values.

We live in a culture of techno-isolation: The nation's favourite television programmes are soaps such as *Coronation Street*, *Neighbours*, *East Enders*, and *Home and Away*; all of which focus on community and life together. Be it the Queen Vic pub in Albert Square, or the Rovers Return in Coronation Street, we are drawn to plots that focus on life together – where 'a neighbour is a footstep away.'

The challenge for the Church, in a lonely and increasingly busy culture, is to provide a sense of warmth and community rather than just holding religious services where songs are sung, liturgy is expressed and information is gathered – and where the only relationships people experience are 'close encounters of the evangelical kind'. Jesus treated all persons with respect regardless of their nationality, race, gender, age, physical condition or economic status (eg. Luke 15:1–32 and John 4:1–26).

"The gospel of Christ knows of no religion, but social religion. No holiness, but social holiness."

– John Wesley

THE GOSPEL ACCORDING TO JOHN

John Drane, a professor at Aberdeen University, was challenged by Paul's bold incarnational approach to evangelism.

He studied Paul's strategy in Athens, where Paul boldly used the pagan 'altar to the unknown god' to illustrate a point and preach the gospel of Jesus. Rather than condemning the Athenians for their ridiculous paganism, Paul used an occult object to declare the truth.

John began to ask the question – where are the 'altars to the unknown gods' in Britain today. He didn't have to search far for the answer – every Sunday 'psychic fairs' are held around the country. People gather to sell crystals, read tarot cards, and taste a host of other occultic practices.

Christians will quickly affirm the obvious danger of these practices – but the fact remains that these fairs are gathering points for people who are seeking spiritual reality, even if they are looking in the wrong places. John rented a stall at a psychic fair and began to share the good news of Jesus in a variety of creative ways – including the use of tarot cards. John discovered that the tarot uses a number of biblical images – so he advertised a seminar on 'the hidden meaning of the tarot' and using cards like 'death' and 'the hanged man' he shared the message of Jesus.

Numbers of people have come to faith in Christ as a result.

THE INTERNET ALTAR: SURFING THE NET WITH SANTER

City Gate Church in Southampton launched a web-site in September 1995 aimed at university students. They advertised it through beer mats based on the Guinness advert slogan 'Pure Genius' and in newspapers. They also registered with the main internet search engines.

The response was very positive. The audience mainly consisted of students, all of whom had free access via the university server. During term time the site has been busy.

As a church with around 120 adults, over a year they have seen 70 students come along on a fairly regular basis, all of whom are on e-mail, plus a further 50 or so who are on the list. It took Mike Santer, part of the leadership team, around four days to create the site.

CHURCH AS COMMUNITY

We must consider how our churches help:

- single people to embrace their singleness.
- older people to cope with the ageing process.
- children to feel valued and included.
- women to understand the 'battle of the sexes'.
- people with disabilities to be included and enjoy their abilities.
- unemployed/retired not to feel useless or inferior.
- families of prisoners to feel accepted.

Community will not be achieved by the proliferation of church meetings, but by their reduction. It will require diverse shapes and rhythms. It will involve interaction at many levels, and for various purposes.

JESUS THE EVANGELIST

> A church in West Sussex recently cancelled their Sunday meeting in order to plant flower bulbs around the city at the request of the local council. They did so in an endeavour to be good news to their community, seeing that as more important than holding a service that morning. What do you think of their decision?

"... that they may see your good deeds and praise your Father in heaven."

– Matt 5:16

WWW http//web link

Volunteers at work on a project in Belfast.

www.habitat.org

Habitat for Humanity International

book .link

The Social Context of the New Testament – Derek Tidball, Paternoster Press

Incarnation 4: Words and works together

Jesus did not separate the work of showing practical kindness and care for people from the words and messages that he declared – words and action met together in him.

Historically the Church has been content to settle for one half of the Great Commission – either spiritual dynamic or social impact. Yet in every visitation of the Holy Spirit, God has joined the two together.

John Stott in 1984 said: "One of the most notable features of the worldwide evangelical movement during the last ten to 15 years has been the recovery of our temporarily mislaid social conscience. For approximately 50 years (c1920–70) evangelical Christians were preoccupied with the task of defending the historic biblical faith against the attacks of theological liberalism, and reacting against its 'social gospel'. But now we are convinced that God has given us social as well as evangelistic responsibilities in his world. Yet the half-century of neglect has put us far behind in this area"

Social involvement and the Great Commission (Matt 28:16–20) contains five critical factors.

1. Proclamation: Telling primarily, but also explaining and demonstrating good news.

2. Plantation: A viable kingdom community within reach of everyone pursuing the reign of Christ in every area of life.

3. Preparation: Teaching and training church members in order to produce informed disciples and competent leadership; and teaching and training across society to introduce and affirm a Christian world view on every subject and area of life.

4. Penetration: Entering every sphere of life and work within society. We are all 'full-time' workers whatever our career/responsibilities.

HABITAT FOR HUMANITY

Habitat for Humanity International is a nonprofit, ecumenical Christian organization dedicated to eliminating substandard housing and homelessness worldwide and to making adequate, affordable shelter a matter of conscience and action. Habitat was founded 24 years ago on the conviction that every man, woman and child should have a simple, decent, affordable place to live in dignity and safety. Volunteers work with future homeowners to build or renovate houses, which are then sold to partner families at no profit, with no interest charged on the 15–20 year mortgage. The money from the sale of each house goes into a revolving Fund for Humanity, to support future building projects.

The work of Habitat is a partnership founded on common ground that bridges theological differences – everyone can use the hammer as an instrument to manifest God's love. Habitat Founder Millard Fuller says, "We may disagree on all sorts of other things, but we can agree on the idea of building homes with God's people in need, and in doing so using biblical economics: no profit and no interest."

US President Jimmy Carter was deeply committed to social justice and basic human rights. His involvement with Habitat began in 1984, when the former president led a work group to New York City to help renovate a six-story building with 19 families in need of decent, affordable shelter. The Jimmy Carter Work Project has been an internationally recognized event of HFHI ever since.

"Habitat has successfully removed the stigma of charity by substituting it with a sense of partnership. " Carter says. "The people who will live in the homes work side-by-side with the volunteers, so they feel very much that they are on an equal level."

Since its founding in 1976 by Millard and his wife, Habitat has built and rehabilitated some 80,000 houses with families in need, becoming a true world leader in addressing the issues of poverty housing.

The concept was born at Koinonia Farm, a small, interracial, Christian farming community founded in 1942 outside of Americus, Georgia, by farmer and biblical scholar Clarence Jordan. The Fullers first visited Koinonia in 1965, having recently left a successful business in Montgomery, Alabama, and all the trappings of an affluent lifestyle to begin a new life of Christian service.

At Koinonia, Jordan and Fuller developed the concept of "partnership housing" – where those in need of adequate shelter would work side by side with volunteers to build simple, decent houses.

The houses would be built with no profit added and no interest charged. Building would be financed by a revolving Fund for Humanity. The fund's money would come from the new homeowners' house payments, donations and no-interest loans provided by supporters and money earned by fund-raising activities. The monies in the Fund for Humanity would be used to build more houses.

Habitat's economic philosophy is based upon what Fuller calls the "economics of Jesus." The no-profit, no-interest components of the program come from a passage in the Bible (Ex 22:25) that says someone lending money to the poor should not act as a creditor and charge interest.

"I see life as both a gift and a responsibility," Fuller says. "My responsibility is to use what God has given me to help his people in need."

HOW TO CHANGE THE WORLD

Ideas have the power to change whole societies. Nelson Mandela is a great example of this. Although a whole political structure might resist his concepts and have the power to remove him from the public domain, yet the ideas of a free and equal society for the majority black and minority white population of South Africa ultimately prevailed.

As ideas get disseminated, shared at a popular level, expressed by media and so forth, they eventually become adopted as the norms of human behaviour. Initially an idea has nothing but its inherent energy to convince people. Hence ideas that will eventually influence nations require a group of highly committed people. They can expect to pay a high price to implement them.

John Wesley produced a tract against slavery. It was laughed at in its day. However a young Wilberforce read the tract and spoke to Wesley. In 40 years of public service Wilberforce brought an abolition bill before Parliament 18 times. It was finally passed into law three weeks after Wilberforce died. This is the process and price by which ideas shape nations.

Taking Action – Roy McCloughry, InterVarsity Press

5. Participation: In decision making, planning for the life of the local community and society at large through the realm of business, leisure, social service, politics, finance, education, home, relationships, etc.

Some organizations have opted to concentrate more on works than words – and have sadly been accused of being 'not evangelical enough' as a result.

What are the challenges for our church in the new century? And how can we respond?

What can we learn from the examples of others who have put their faith into action and changed their communities, or even impacted the wider international community?

www.alpha.org.uk

Incarnation 5: Patience and peaceful evangelism

Process as well as crisis

A recent report discovered that only 31 per cent of Christians interviewed could report a datable or "point" conversion. Even in evangelical churches only 37 per cent were converted in this way. Most were gradually converted. What are the implications for evangelistic methods?

www.christianityexplained.org

Do we need to make more space for people to 'take a look' at the claims and invitation of Jesus without pressure?

The phenomenal success of the Alpha course suggests that a less-pressurised approach to evangelism is the way forward.

www.yway.org

A course called 'Christianity Explained' has been developed by Michael Bennett in Australia.

The course offers an opportunity to look at the Christian faith with the guarantee that:

- it will not be assumed that those attending the course know nothing about Christianity
- no one will be asked to read anything aloud
- no one will be asked to pray
- no one will be asked to answer questions.

Beyond Belief? – Peter Meadows and Joseph Steinberg, Word

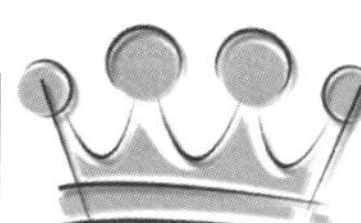

EVEN MORE RADICAL

Roy McCloughry in 1996 wrote: "... until recently, evangelicals thought of their task as engagement with the personal agendas of 'individuals' whose personal response to Christ was the only way in which the church could hope to influence society. As more people became Christians so society would become more Christian.

"In this view there was a tendency to see anything which was not overtly religious as 'belonging to the world' and thus, in turn, ensured that it was either disregarded or vilified. This atomistic view has declined in recent years, not because evangelicals have lessened their commitment to the transformation of the person through the work of Christ, but because they have seen that Christianity offers a far more radical and comprehensive view of salvation history than can be described by such means.

"Now evangelicals frequently talk about engaging with contemporary culture, the partnership of evangelism with social action, the necessity to address political issues, and the concept of the Christian mind as part of an agenda that seeks not only to preserve evangelical unity and integrity but also to influence contemporary culture to favour Christian norms and behaviour."

A NEW CHALLENGE

Derek Tidball gives a perceptive assessment of the current situation in a recent book, which concludes with a challenge to the evangelical community:

"As far as social action is concerned evangelicals are on the road to recovery. They are learning that the test of right doctrine is right practice... . Older evangelicals have fears, perhaps because of their memory of the social gospel movement, which strayed from the authentic gospel into a gospel akin to socialism. They question whether it is possible to hold at one and the same time both the preaching of personal salvation and social transformation without the latter taking over the former. But they must be encouraged to look to an earlier generation of evangelicals for their model, rather than to evangelicals of the earlier 20th century. Earlier in the 19th century, both in Anglican evangelicalism centred around Clapham and in the revivalist evangelicalism of the United States, evangelicals maintained a balance worth a vigorous commitment both to evangelism and social reform in which neither was compromised."

> **?** "Heaven and hell is in the balance. A little pressure is therefore appropriate in our evangelistic presentations." Comment.

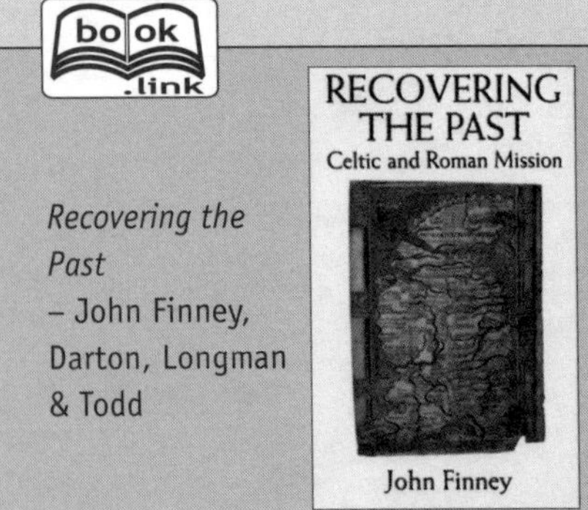

Recovering the Past – John Finney, Darton, Longman & Todd

> **?** Has your church tried running an Alpha course? If so, please report on the results/ strengths/weaknesses.

Final statement:

We have good news, vitally relevant news to share with our post-Christian culture. Perhaps there is an opportunity for us to live and speak the gospel with a clarity and freshness that has not been available for many years. Evangelism is not about church growth or expansion. It is about people meeting Jesus.

As we discover more of what it is to really live rather than exist, there will be others around us who will want to discover the 'key' to our quality of life.

The Early Church didn't grow because of the spiritual gifts of Christians such as speaking in tongues. Nor because Christianity was such a palatable doctrine (it's most unpalatable). It grew because they had discovered the secret of community. Sometimes, they did not have to lift a finger to evangelize. Someone would be walking down a back alley in Corinth or Ephesus and see a group of people talking about the strangest things. They made no sense, but gave off the scent of love. The onlooker would start to drift farther down the alley; only to be pulled back thinking, I don't have the slightest idea what these people are talking about, but whatever it is, I want part of it.

The Signature of Jesus – Brennan Manning, Multnomah Press

Beware the trap of focusing on the common superficialities of other Christians around us. We note that we are no better, or worse, than them and so continue to drift through our 'Christian' life, following Jesus at a considerable distance. The challenge is to hear Jesus say to us, as he did to Peter, "What is that to you? You must follow me" – John 21:22.

"... if we preferred to be faithful rather than successful, the walls of indifference to Jesus Christ would crumble. A handful of us could be ignored by society; but hundreds, thousands, millions of such servants would overwhelm the world. Christians filled with the

PEACEFUL EVANGELISM

Evangelism has too often been associated with coercion and pressure. Vinoth Ramachandra says evangelism can be confident but must also be humble: "Since the gospel announces the sheer grace of God towards unworthy sinners, it can be commended to others only in a spirit of humility. It is all of grace. This forbids me from thinking of the gospel as my possession and of evangelism as a matter of demonstrating the superiority of my 'religion' over all others."

Humble evangelism may include 'asking forgiveness from others' for perversions of the gospel and atrocities committed in the name of Christ, as well as offering divine forgiveness to others. It will certainly involve more listening than talking, starting where people are rather than where the Church is.

John Finney summarises the main features of this understanding of evangelism: "It goes where people are and listens, binds together prayer and truth, celebrates the goodness and complexity of life as well as judging the sinfulness of evil, and sees truth as something to be done and experienced as well as to be intellectually believed. It walks in humility."

authenticity, commitment and generosity of Jesus would be the most spectacular sign in the history of the human race. The call of Jesus is revolutionary. If we implemented it, we would change the world in a few months." – Brennan Manning, *The Signature of Jesus.*

With these words, Emile Leger left his mansion in Montreal to live in a leper colony in Africa: "The time for talking is over."

EXTRA

THE BANQUET CONTINUES

In the closing words of our Study Guide, "The time for talking is over." Now is the moment of truth. Will we live a life of radical obedience to Christ – or will we just talk about it?

The end of Spring Harvest marks the start of an adventure, putting into practice the things we have learnt at our banquet.

The following pages provide four weeks of daily notes with a Bible passage to read and some ideas to help you work at turning theory and learning into practical reality.

Why not use these notes to help you start to take the bold steps that God is challenging us all to take, for his glory and his kingdom?

Acknowledgement

These notes were specially written for the Spring Harvest 2000 Study Guide by Neil Dougall, a Church of Scotland minister. They are supplied by Scripture Union, who produce daily Bible reading notes for adults. Details are available from Scripture Union on 01908 856000.
Or order direct from SU Mail Order, PO Box 764, Oxford OX4 5FJ; tel: 01865 716880.

WEEK 1

JESUS AT THE CENTRE

INTRODUCTION

Rather than one day a week, Christ is Lord of all our life. Our faith needs to shape all that we are and do, 7 days a week, 24 hours a day.

In our readings this week, we reflect on what that means for different aspects of life.

Day 1 Family life

Natalie sulks in her room because Mum says she can only see her boyfriend at weekends. Darren's grounded; he longs to be out playing footie; instead he stares grimly at the TV. Mum and Dad now live apart. They meet to talk about the children and end up arguing. Welcome to UK Family 2000!

Read Eph 6:1-4

With God's help we can begin to put the broken pieces of family together again. By his grace our faith will shape our family life and help us build lasting relationships. This passage offers one important perspective by turning a basic assumption on its head. For while it's common today to talk about *my rights*, the passage talks instead about my *responsibilities* and the rights of *others*.

A child's responsibility is to honour their parents. I wonder what that might mean now for Natalie and Darren, and what it will mean for them in 10 years and 30 years time?

Parents are not told to demand obedience from their children, rather, not to be overbearing. Is that how Natalie and Darren felt Mum and Dad were? What advice would you give them about how to be firm, yet gracious to their children?

Prayer:

Family life is often painful. Take a few moments to bring to God your hurts and disappointments about your own family experience – being a child, being a parent, being …

Day 2 Working life

Read Eph 6:5–9

In the film Snow White, the seven dwarves set out each morning singing cheerfully, 'Hi ho, hi ho, it's off to work we go.' Dream on! For many people work is drudgery. At best it's tolerable, at worst awful. Yet this is nothing compared to the working life of a slave at the time Ephesians was written.

Paul's instruction was radical. Instead of 'exploit every loophole you can find' it's 'do your best at all times.' What revolutionary perspective was Paul bringing to working life (v7)?

All of life is a sacrament. Every chore can be holy. No task is too small for God's care. Every single thing I do, can be brought to him. So a slave can see his daily chores as service to Christ the King. The work itself is no different, but Christ gives it dignity and value, changing it beyond recognition.

You are not a slave, but you may hate your work. Indeed the work you do may not even be classed as 'work' because you aren't paid for it. But Jesus has a different perspective. He says, 'I care about the mundane things you have to do today. Serve and worship me as you do them.'

Prayer:

Father, I bring you the tasks which lie before me today. Help me to do them all for you and to remember that even if others neither notice nor care, you do.

Day 3 Domestic life

Read Luke 10:38–41

In my house domestic details constantly create friction. The issues are petty – about tidying up and washing up; and the cries insistent – 'it's not fair.' What I find astonishing about Mary and Martha's story is that it's there in the first place. Four verses of Holy Scripture are devoted to a minor domestic squabble between two sisters. Why has an everyday 'unimportant' incident been preserved for all time?

Domestic life matters to God. He has dignified housework by preserving this story. The petty details of our lives are not insignificant to him. If the hairs on our head are numbered, so are the dirty dishes waiting by the kitchen sink.

But domestic life can get out of hand too. Martha was trying to serve Jesus, but her service left her upset and hassled. Some people, like Martha, prefer relating to Jesus through action, others, like Mary, through reflection. But keeping the right balance can be difficult. Jesus said Mary had 'chosen what's better,' which suggests that Martha's activism was harming, not helping her relationship with Jesus.

Prayer:

Thank God that he cares about hoovering, washing up, paying bills and doing the garden. But he cares even more about your love relationship with him.

Day 4 Shopping

Read Prov 20:14-23

One survey found that Americans spend 6 hours a week shopping; Britain isn't far behind. A recent TV ad by a high street chemist described shopping as retail therapy. Many people would list shopping as one of their hobbies. This passage in Proverbs has some pithy sayings about shopping, designed to make us stop and think.

Everyone loves a bargain, but verse 14 makes us consider the other people involved. Sometimes we need to ask, how does the bargain I've found affect the shop workers, the coffee pickers, or the sweat shop workers?

Our society is fixated by material values. Something is worth what its price tag says. Verse 15 reminds us that it's non-material things which are really valuable. 'It doesn't matter as long as you don't get caught' is a contemporary motto. Verse 17 points up the need for honesty in all we say and do – which includes our shopping.

Shops can cheat too and God clearly isn't happy with this either (v 23). But before we relax, what about when we sold our house, our car, or even our junk at a car boot sale? How honest were we?

Prayer:

In a world obsessed with having and getting, reflect on Matt 6:33. Why not try and memorise it and recall it a few times during the day?

Day 5 Leisure

'Young people can live a clean life by obeying your word.' (Psalm 119:9 CEV). No matter your age, ask God to help you meditate on his Word today, that you may serve him well.

Read Phil 4:8,9

Last year The Sun newspaper had a billboard advert which read: 'Drink, drugs, violence, corruption and vice. And that's just the sports pages.' In a society which delights in the mucky depths humans descend to, God's people are, quite consciously and deliberately, to be different. God has given us a wide range of leisure opportunities. They are his good gifts and we receive them with thanks. But if we are not to be killjoys, equally we are to choose wisely. Paul urges us to opt for what is wholesome and worthy, to select what is good and right.

How does your leisure – viewing, net-surfing, reading, sport-playing – appear when filtered through the grid of verse 8? Being a Christian is not just about nice ideas and enjoyable worship. It includes putting what we've heard into practice in the ordinary things of daily life (v 9).

Prayer:

So why not spend a few minutes, talking to God about those ordinary things and asking for his help to live for him in them?

Day 6 Respecting others

Titles and protocol bug me. When people ask whether to call me 'Rev' or 'Mr', I say, 'Neil will do just fine'. I'm glad society has ditched many conventions, but the downside is that sometimes we don't know how to treat others. Paul's advice to Timothy contains some timeless principles.

Read 1 Tim 5:1,2

Timothy was a youngish man given leadership responsibility in church. He didn't just have to relate to people of all ages, he had to correct, teach and counsel them. In a nutshell, Paul's advice was to imagine other people are members of your own family. Treat them as you would your own father or mother, brother or sister.

Family life today though, can be so messy that this needs spelling out.

1. Respect age. Age does not equal wisdom, but older people have seen more than most of us have. Grey hair should be respected, not despised.
2. Don't bully those not as strong as you. Jesus is the strongest person there ever was, but he won the world through love and kindness, not force and manipulation.
3. The opposite sex is to be treated with purity. All kinds of sexual behaviour are accepted by society. God's people are different. Our relationships with the other sex will demonstrate this.

These principles apply not just to leaders but to all of us in all our relationships.

Prayer:

Talk to God about the one which you find most difficult.

Day 7 Being made new

'Anyone who belongs to Christ is a new person. The past is forgotten and everything is new.' (2 Corinthians 5:17 CEV). Thank God for this. Ask him to show you more of what it means.

Read Col 3:5-14

Can you recall a time when you were doing a really dirty job, eg decorating, gardening, fixing something? You had to go out, so you changed. Try and create a mental picture of before and after.

Paul uses this idea here. The 'before' picture, that is life without Christ, is verses 5 to 9. As you read these verses again, is there one feature that is or was particularly true of you?

The 'after' picture, that is life in Christ, is verses 12 to 14. The way we relate to other people is to be as different now as our good gear is from our dirty overalls. The key quality in all of this is love. As we show God's-kind-of-love to each other, all the other pieces will fall into place. Think about the people you expect to meet today or tomorrow. How might you show 'compassion, kindness, humility, gentleness and patience' to them?

Prayer:

Father,
I can't do this on my own.
Give me your love for others
that I might treat them today
as you want me to. Amen.

WEEK 2

JESUS THE DISCIPLER

INTRODUCTION

Discipleship may be born or renewed at Spring Harvest, but it's a lifelong journey rather than a momentary commitment. Discipleship involves the changing of character and attitudes. The first disciples discovered this, often quite painfully, as we see as we focus for a few days on their walk with Jesus recorded in Luke 9.

Day 1 How far have you come?

Read Luke 9:18–20

I live in Edinburgh and my in-laws live 300 miles away in Lincolnshire. We visit three times a year. Our children look forward greatly to these visits, counting off the days and even the hours, until we set off. But as soon as we do, the start is forgotten. Now it's, 'How far have we gone?' 'When will we get there?'

For Peter and the other disciples this was a big day. Jesus' question about people's opinion shows popular opinion was split over his identity. Was Jesus wondering, 'Had the penny had dropped for the disciples yet?' Peter spoke for the others, expressing what they were privately wondering. Everyone was thrilled when Jesus nodded his head. Was there a round of high-fives, or discreet thumbs up? 'Good shot, Peter.'

As we make commitments to Christ we are charged with enthusiasm and excitement. Confessions like Peter's are special and important. We remember these moments years later; but they can also be over-rated. Peter was about to discover, this was just the journey *to* faith. The journey *of* faith was about to begin. As we'll see this week, there were to be plenty of hard knocks along the way.

Reflect on your own journey of faith. Was there a classic beginning like Peter's? What's happened since? Is anything happening at the moment? How far have you gone … or are you stuck? Talk to God about these things.

Meditation:

Meditate on Phil 3:12–14

Day 2 The suffering's in the large print

I felt I got stung last month by my bank. 'Only 1% charge for your Travel Money' said the leaflet – but I hadn't checked the small print which pointed out there was a minimum charge. I hate that. The sum involved was small, but I felt I'd been cheated.

Is there a small print section in the Discipleship brochure?

Read Luke 9:21–27 to find out

We live in a society that tells us the key to life is grabbing for yourself, but Jesus says it's letting go. The TV is full of tips to avoid hardship. Jesus says, choose the path of suffering. The papers tell us how to make the most of life, but Jesus says that it's only by saving your life that you can get it. This is discipleship. Jesus said suffering, hardship and death would happen to him, and it did. Yet has there ever been a more rounded and fulfilled person on this planet?

Jim Elliot, a missionary in South America, was killed by the people he was taking the gospel to. He memorably said, 'He is no fool who gives what he cannot keep, to gain what he cannot lose.'

Are you grabbing for yourself or letting go?

Prayer:

Lord, I don't like suffering or hardship any more than others do. Give me courage to believe Jesus and to follow him on the road to the cross. Amen.

Day 3 Mountain top highs

Read Luke 9:28-36

Bible teaching in the morning, fellowship all day long, Celebrations at night. At Spring Harvest we practically overdosed on worship and the sense of God's presence. Peter, James and John would have been entirely at home. Consider what they saw and heard on the mountain top with Jesus. I'm sure that they must have felt overpowered as they were touched by the presence of God.

With their physical senses they encountered the Lord God of the universe. It was awesome, spine-tingling, a mind-blowing event. Peter wanted to be helpful. He suggested setting up camp there to try to prolong the experience, but all that remark did was to show how far out of his depth he was.

The mountain top was Jesus' gift to Peter, James and John. They didn't ask for it or expect it. It just happened. From time to time God gives us special experiences of his presence to help us on the path of discipleship.

When he does, make the most of them, but don't try to hang onto them.

Prayer:

Have you been the mountain top, in the wilderness, or somewhere in between this last week? Ask God to assure you of the reality of his presence, wherever you're going, whatever you're doing.

Day 4 A double whammy

Read Luke 9:37–42

Can you remember an occasion recently when you felt left out? Everyone else was invited to a party, a meal or a meeting and you weren't. Did the other disciples feel unwanted and battle against a sense of injustice as they watched Jesus disappear up the mountain with Peter, James and John?
Opportunity knocks, ministry is requested. 'Can you help my only son?' It's a double whammy. They're not good enough to climb the mountain and they're not spiritual enough to heal the boy. I feel the taste of failure in my mouth as I stand in the shoes of the nine. You know how they felt, because you've been there too.
What does Jesus say and do, (vs 41, 42)? The healing is great, the rebuke difficult. The nine had tried their hardest, yet Jesus says a lack of faith is the problem. That's hard to take - hard when you do your best and your best isn't good enough.
I learn here that falling on my face and getting up again is part of discipleship. Following Jesus includes many things which I don't understand and which leave me feeling resentful and even bitter. It's then I hear the voice of Jesus, 'Are you still coming with me? Are you still willing to trust me? Do you still believe I love you and want what's best for you?' *What's your answer?*

Prayer:

Take time to talk to Jesus about the disappointments, the heartaches and the failures you may be experiencing.

Day 6 Confronting prejudice

Read Luke 9:49–55

Prejudice is alive in the church today. John was guilty of the narrow mindedness found among many Christians. 'He doesn't do things in exactly the same way as we do. He can't be a real Christian' (verse 49). Paul says, 'If you confess with your mouth. 'Jesus is Lord' and believe in your heart that God raised him from the dead, you will be saved.' (Romans 10:9) Is your fellowship based on this, or are you guilty of adding to the gospel?
Prejudice is alive in the world today. 'We hate anyone going to Jerusalem. Don't come here' (v 52). James and John were incensed. 'Fry them alive, Lord!' How do you respond when you encounter prejudice? Do you lash out in anger, or turn away as Jesus did? Discipleship involves both confronting the prejudice in our own hearts and turning the other cheek when we are the victims of it.

Prayer:

Some issues to mull over.

? What sorts of prejudice are found in your fellowship?

? Is it possible to turn away (as Jesus did) but still confront prejudice?

Put another way, is it possible to turn away from anger, but still to tell prejudicial people, 'What you are doing is wrong'? If so, when should you do this?

Day 5 Centred on self

'Jesus, being in very nature God, did not consider equality with God something to be grasped, but made himself nothing.' (Philippians 2:6).
Pause and reflect on what Jesus surrendered.

Read Luke 9:44–48

'I am going to die.' Like water off a duck's back, Jesus' words bounce off the disciples. All they're interested in is, 'Who's going to be top dog?' One-upmanship is a universal human disease. Some folk are blatant; they look for, they ask for, they try to take the best seat. Other folk are more subtle: they manipulate, they attract attention by being humble. Appearing to avoid recognition, secretly they seek it.
Children were near the bottom of the pile, not at the centre of the universe, in Jesus' day. That's where Jesus placed himself and where we've to place ourselves. It's not easy, because self is in the promotion business. It's not easy, because often we fail to see how addicted to greatness we are.

Prayer:

Lord Jesus
take the scales from my eyes
so that I see how strong self really is.
Help me today to have the attitude you had
so that in humility,
I consider others better than myself.
Amen.

Day 7 To give up or go on?

Read Luke 9:57–62

I got a free computer magazine through the post one day — a taster, to entice me to subscribe to it. I enjoyed reading it, but didn't take out the subscription. Discipleship begins by tasting but as it continues it touches and shapes every part of our lives. Jesus said, 'If you come with me, you have to be prepared to give your all' (v 23). Three blokes along the road hadn't grasped this. Why did they choose to stay behind?
Their reasons sound plausible - excuses always do. But was his father elderly, let alone ill or even dead? What sort of farewell was planned? Jesus cuts through the flannel. 'Make your mind up. Are you committing yourself totally to me, or are you not?'
Its no different now. Being a Christian is not a soft option for weak characters. It's a tough choice that involves all we have and are. Jesus says, 'Follow me!' In my faltering way, with many setbacks and defeats, I'm going. How about you?

Prayer:

Lord Jesus,
I want to journey with you through life,
but I know how weak my will is,
it won't be long before I think about giving up.
Help me by your Holy Spirit
to live for you each day
and to go on, through thick and thin.
Amen.

WEEK 3

JESUS AND PRAYER

INTRODUCTION

Spiritual folk are those who are so heavenly minded that they are no earthly use? That description doesn't fit Jesus. Never was there a person who was both so absorbed with his heavenly Father and so involved with the material world. Luke's portrait of Jesus shows a person who seems to have prayed all the time. In not a few passages, Luke has added a reference to Jesus praying in places where it's not present in Matthew and Mark. Jesus gives us an example of how to balance prayer and action.

Day 1 The presence of God

'Come near to God and he will come near to you.' (James 4:8). Take time to respond to this invitation and promise.

Read Luke 3:21,22

God is with us everywhere and at all times, though most of the time we are unaware of this. When we deliberately seek him, we are much more aware of his presence. It's not a hard and fast rule — barren prayer times are experienced by all Christians. Yet it's generally true — as we come near to God, we sense his nearness to us.

Jesus' baptism in the Jordan was a momentous event marking the start of his ministry. Any hesitations he may have been experiencing were banished. God clearly and explicitly gave his stamp of approval. The power of God, through the Holy Spirit, visibly came down on Jesus. Look at what Jesus was doing when this happened (v 21). Jesus was always aware of his Father's presence, yet he still prayed. I suspect that in those moments this awareness was much stronger. That this visible and dramatic encounter with the Father happened at one of these times is no coincidence.

What space have you created in your regular routine to draw near to God?

Prayer:

Father, help me to make space and time in my busy life to turn from other things and be with you. Amen.

Day 2 Testing times

Read Luke 4:1–11

Prayer means engaging with God. It includes speaking to God but is more than this. Often prayer has been separated from reading the Bible. Yet, if we are doing it the right way, reading the Bible is prayer. We encounter God through the words on the page and make our response to him.

Straight after the baptism, Jesus went to a lonely area. With his Father's endorsement ringing in his ears, he walked straight into a massive battle with the devil. Three times, in three quite different ways, and appealing to three different desires, the devil tried to lead Jesus astray.

What was the thing Jesus used on each occasion to blunt the force of temptation? Quoting Scripture, Jesus was able to remind himself where right and wrong lay. Quoting Scripture, Jesus found reserves of spiritual strength to do what was right. Quoting Scripture Jesus experienced his Father's presence which he needed so badly.

Temptation is inevitable; we can't escape it. Prayer is vital for facing it. Prayer, which includes absorbing God's word and responding to him through it, strengthens and prepares us for battle. The old idea of a regular daily time for reading God's Word and responding to him was an attempt to take this seriously. If that is a pattern you have rejected or never tried, ask, 'What am I doing to make sure I'm ready for battle when it comes?'

Prayer:

Father, help me to absorb your word and to engage with you, regularly, as Jesus did. Amen.

Day 3 Recharging the batteries

'He who dwells in the shelter of the Most High will rest in the shadow of the Almighty. I will say of the Lord, "He is my refuge and my fortress, my God in whom I trust".' – Psa 91:1,2

Read Luke 4:38–42

People queuing for hours to have him touch them. People travelling for miles just to see him. Jesus was riding the crest of a wave, but seemed determined to get off it. Look at his unusual response to popular acclaim (v 43).

I like being popular. I like being appreciated; the thought of people travelling for miles to hear me preach makes me drool. But not Jesus. Somehow, he kept his focus and remained unswayed by popular expectation. Verse 42 explains why. Spending time with God kept him from either staying too long with one activity or running away in exhaustion.

Ministry is draining. The more drained we are the harder it becomes to think clearly. Jesus could give out so much because he took in all the time from his Father. He carved out space to be with his Father, which meant he could engage with daily life in God's power.

Activism and inactivity are two traps Christians often fall into. How's the balance in your life?

Prayer:

Father, help me to draw apart with you and then to engage in daily life with your energy just as Jesus did. Amen.

Day 4 Decision time

Read Luke 6:12–16

I find discovering God's will for particular situations I face difficult. Other Christians I know say the same thing. Guidance is tricky.

Jesus faced a crucial decision. Out of the many hundreds who followed him, twelve were to be recruited for in-depth training. The future of the church rested on this — choosing the right people was essential.

Today there are decisions before you — perhaps small ones, but maybe ones which will affect the rest of your life. What did Jesus do that helped him get it right (v 12)?

I'm certain he didn't repeat the same prayer a thousand times that night. I doubt that he ran through a huge list of names as hour followed hour. I suspect Jesus was simply quiet with his Father. He rested in his presence saying very little. When decision time came, he knew.

Knowing God's will comes from knowing God. Prayer is more than asking God questions, it's being intimate and quiet with him. The more we do this, the more likely it is that the ideas in our minds will be God's.

O sabbath rest by Galilee!
O calm of hills above,
Where Jesus knelt to share with Thee
The silence of eternity,
Interpreted by love! – *JG Whittier*

Prayer:

Father, help me to experience this too.

Day 5 Prayer is attractive

Read Luke 11:1–4

At a 'living museum' one year, we watched a blacksmith at work. Rods of iron were heated, twisted, cooled and cut. Before our eyes a decorative gate began to take shape.

Watching an expert at work, we say to ourselves, 'I want to be like you.' If the expert is approachable, we ask them to teach us. If the expert is a good teacher, we get the best help possible.

Over the months Jesus disciples had seen how important prayer was to him. This day they said, 'We want to be like you. Please show us.'

The prayer Jesus taught is to be used in two ways. First, as a prayer we say word for word, and I would encourage you to say it every day. Second, it's a pattern for all our praying. It tells us who we pray to and how we should pray:

It's to our Father, and this can be our approach:

Praise is where we begin.
Asking comes next.
Saying sorry must happen.
Safety is where it ends.

(From the first letters you get the word *PASS*)

Prayer:

Are you attracted to prayer? If not, why might that be? If you pray regularly, is the pattern of the Lord's Prayer reflected in this?

Day 6 Keep at it!

'The Lord is faithful to all his promises and loving towards all he has made.' – Psa 145:13

Take a moment to thank God for his faithfulness.

Read Luke 11:5–12

The phone rang in the middle of the night — the police to say that lights had been reported at our church! Its awful when my beauty sleep is disturbed! We can understand how the man in Jesus' story felt. Look at what made it more of an ordeal for him (v 7).

Jesus' point is not that God is reluctant to help as the man in the story was. Rather, if even when its an ordeal to help, people do so, how much will our Father in heaven respond to our prayers.

But there's more. The traveller had to keep asking. By this, Jesus suggests that we need to persist in prayer. He doesn't explain why, just encourages us to keep on. We have his promises; first, that God responds to our asking (vs 9,10) and secondly, that God is good and committed to our welfare (vs 11–13).

Prayer:

Is there a part of Jesus' promise that you need particularly to take hold of? Ask God to help you believe and to respond with patient but persevering prayer.

Day 7 Prayer and struggle

In a voice filled with remorse, a friend says, 'I knew it was wrong. I knew I should stop. But something was driving me on. I couldn't turn away. Now look at the mess my life is in.' I've been there … more often than I care to admit. So has Jesus, but in his case it played out differently.

Read Luke 22:39–46

Jesus' arrest and crucifixion were hours away. A quick exit from Jerusalem would have avoided this. Jesus found this 'easy' option very attractive and Luke shows us how hard he fought the temptation. As you reread verses 42 to 44, what feelings do you experience?

I've never sweated blood. I've given into temptation long before it gets as tough as this. But I need not have. Heb 4:15 says, Jesus 'has been tempted in every way, just as we are — yet was without sin.' My experience is different from Jesus' because I'm like the disciples. When I need to wrestle in prayer, I fall asleep … or turn on the TV … or turn to an 'urgent' task. Jesus, facing the full assault of hell, kept praying till the battle was won.

Prayer:

Father, when temptation is strongest, that's often when I least want to pray. Help me to be more like Jesus, to take hold of you and to refuse to let go until the struggle is over.

WEEK 4

JESUS THE EVANGELIST

INTRODUCTION

Sharing faith is a thread running through the New Testament, but it keeps changing colour! Far from being a single activity, a great breadth of styles and details are recorded. Each of us is different, and God expects us to share our faith in a way which is natural for the kind of person he made us.

Day 1 More than a pun!

Read Matt 4:18–22

It's a clever play on words — fishermen become fishers of men. Instead of bringing fish from the lake into their boat, Andrew and Peter will bring people into the church of Jesus Christ. But it's much more than a pun. It says a great deal about the way God works and the people he uses.

I spent six years at University being prepared for ordination. In Jesus' day Rabbis served an equally long apprenticeship. Peter and Andrew were just fishermen, with no formal training and no professional church qualifications. In their own eyes, they had little to offer Jesus. Do you feel just an ordinary sort of person? Jesus says it doesn't matter. He deliberately uses what they are good at, fishing, to talk about the work he was wanting them to do.

He called twelve ordinary people, and not one professional cleric! Jesus takes ordinary people and, by his Holy Spirit, he makes them extraordinary! In the midst of daily life and using skills we have, he calls us to be his witnesses.

Prayer:

If you feel 'too ordinary' to be of use to Jesus, ask him to show you how special you are to him and how he wants you to serve him.

Day 2 Sharing the story

Read Matt 10:5–9

When someone says, 'You need to share your faith with others.' What do you think is meant by this?

Sending the disciples out, Jesus commanded them:

Tell the story. 'You need to tell people about me and why I came to earth' (v 7);

Do the story. 'When you come across people with problems, show my love by ministering to them in the Spirit's power' (v 8);

Live the story. 'If you are preoccupied with your material needs, no one will listen to you. Trust me,' (v 9).

Christians have spent hours arguing about the priority of preaching, power encounters and practical concern in evangelism. That Jesus should bring speaking, healing and lifestyle into one short address suggests it's not either/or, it's both/and/and. We have to speak with words, show with practical care and live out the good news in our lives, the story that 'God was reconciling the world to himself in Christ' (2 Cor 5:19). Keeping these three in balance is not easy. How well do you think you are doing it?

Action:

Which of the three strands is weakest in your life? Think about how you might address it this week and ask God for his help to do this.

Day 3 Master of the universe

'The Lord reigns, let the earth be glad; let the distant shores rejoice'. – Psa 97:1

Pause and let the reality of God's kingly rule grip you. Praise him!

Read Matt 28:16–20

Jesus claims all authority and sends us to tell others about him. We have been commissioned by the Lord of the Universe to speak on his behalf. Speak then, in his authority, not your own.

The target is all nations. Frontiers of nations, race, language or ideology do not restrict him. What might you do to play your part in this world-wide mission?

It's a vastly ambitious task. Jesus says, 'Don't make converts, make disciples. Don't just tell them the ABCs, teach them to obey all things.' All too often, the church is guilty of setting its target too low. The whole thing sounds absurd. Who does Jesus think he is? That's the whole point. As verses 5 and 6 explain, he is the risen Lord, he has defeated all the powers of evil. His authority and Lordship is not in doubt. He is the Master of the Universe and he invites us to share in his work, in his strength.

Prayer:

Lord Jesus, help me this day to do what I can to share my faith. Amen.

Day 4 Over to you now!

Read Acts 1:6–11

Can you think of an occasion when you expected to be a spectator and suddenly you found you'd been given the main role?
Risen from the dead, Jesus met his disciples. What does their question in verse 6 suggest they were expecting?
It made sense. Jesus had proven his authority, so they expected to spectate while Jesus made the kingdom of God visible on earth. The one thing they weren't sure about was when this was going to happen. 'It's over to you now', was Jesus response. 'I'm not going to restore the kingdom, instead, you will build the church by being my witnesses wherever you go.' The trouble is, we've not grasped this. Too often church is a spectator sport. A few people burn themselves up in the middle while the majority sit in the stand and watch.
Like us, the disciples' response was, 'But Jesus I couldn't do that. I haven't the confidence'. That's okay. By his Spirit he gives us *power*; power to speak about our faith, power to live out our faith, power to get out of the stand and run for ninety minutes. Jesus is saying, 'Over to you now'. What do you say?

Meditation:

'God's Spirit doesn't make cowards out of us. The Spirit gives us love. power, and self-control.' –2 Tim 1:7 CEV

Day 5 Gossiping the Gospel

Read Acts 8:1–8

Philip gets a name check; hundreds, maybe even thousands of others are just referred to in passing. Perhaps in heaven, though, we will find out just how significant they turned out to be. What does verse 4 tell us they did? Philip, as the rest of the chapter shows, was a public speaker. He was able to talk about Jesus to a large group of people. It was a memorable occasion and is recorded in some detail..
Persecution forced God's people to flee from Jerusalem. Wherever they went, they couldn't help talking about how Jesus had changed their lives. In the market place and the wash house, walking along the street and sitting in the sun, they chatted about their faith. Their preaching wasn't done from a soap box, but over a morning cuppa. As hundreds of ordinary folk did this, the gospel spread like wildfire. In some parts of the world, this same pattern is being repeated. It probably happened once upon a time in Britain, and it could happen once again ....

Prayer:

Father, help me to talk about my faith as naturally as I chat about the weather, last night's TV and the football. Amen.

Day 6 Who is the evangelist here?

'We have different gifts, according to the grace given us.' – Rom 12:6
Thank God for making you the unique individual you are, and for the gifts he's given you.

Read Acts 18:24-28.

Pundits reckon Scotland's football team lacks any world class players; its great strength though is its teamwork. Apollos was a world class player. What things does the passage tell us he could have put on his CV?
It's easy to resent people who seem to have all the gifts. They get the attention, they get the results, and we feel like nobodies. But without the backroom staff of Priscilla and Aquila, Apollos would not even have made it to the substitutes' bench because his faith was defective (v 25). Sensitively and wisely, Priscilla and Aquila helped Apollos and gave him the support he needed to exercise his ministry.
Apollos probably won thousands for Christ, but on his own he'd never have been so effective. Are you an Apollos character? Don't overrate your value, you need the body of Christ too. Or do you resent Apollos characters? Don't! God has made you who you are and given you your gifts. Ask him to show you how and where he wants you to serve him.

Reflection:

Rom 12:4–7

Day 7 Come and see!

Read John 1:40–46

A new job, a baby's born, exams are passed — all mean more profit for the phone companies. We like sharing good news.
Andrew met Jesus, and went to find his brother, Peter. Philip met Jesus and went looking for his friend Nathanael. What did Andrew and Philip say (vs 41, 45)? Both acted as witnesses. That is, both of them shared what they had seen with their own eyes and invited the others to come and see for themselves.
Our culture is resistant to being preached at - people do not listen if I try to tell them what they must do or believe. Our culture is intensely interested in the story of someone's life - people's ears prick up when I tell what's happened to me. This is just what Jesus has told us to do. He doesn't ask you to bore your workmates with the doctrine of his substitutionary death. He does ask you to tell your friends how he makes your life different. It's not just telling either, it's living that difference out. The enthusiasm of Andrew and Philip spoke as loudly as their words did.

Prayer:

Father, thank you for the difference you make to my life each day. Help me to share my story sensitively and wisely with those I meet today and tomorrow.

GENERATION 2000+

BRINGING HOPE TO THE REAL ISSUES OF FAMILY LIFE TODAY.

Seminar Notes

GENERATION 2000+

Seminar Notes

Contents

Morning Programme Teaching Series

Special Options

Material for the Generation 2000+ Seminar Notes was written by the speakers and edited by Lisa Curtis at Care for the Family.

Day Two

Emotions – can't live with 'em; can't do without 'em

Our emotions are a fundamental part of us. Positive or negative, they play an essential part in the formation of any relationship and have a powerful effect on what we communicate in those relationships.

Communication is the essence, the life-blood of all relationships, so learning to handle our emotions is vital in communicating effectively.

A relationship with God and with meaningful others is the heart of God's plan for us. Understanding emotions (our own and others) and their effect on our communication is important in deepening our relationship with God, our families, others in the church, those in the workplace and in the community at large.

Emotions

What are they? Feelings are neither 'right' nor 'wrong'.

Thinking soundly about anger and what it is.

How emotions affect us all and understanding their place in our relationships.

Communication

What is it? Why is it important? How is it affected by emotions/feelings? Clear, open communication nurtures relationships and enables them to grow and to deepen.

Relationships

We were created to have a deep, close relationship with God. – Jer 24:7

We were created to have a deep, close relationship with others. – Gen 2:18

Think about your relationships. In which one, most of all, could more open communication lead to a deeper, closer relationship?

Day Three

God-given and powerful

Our emotional needs are God-given and a powerful means of communicating well-being in building relationships. God intends these needs to be met in a relationship with Him and with others, thus removing our aloneness.

When our God-given emotional needs are not met, pain and hurt have many consequences. There are various causes of anger, fear, depression and we can learn ways of handling these. Forgiveness has a key role in releasing negative emotions.

The God of Emotions

There are many references in Scripture to God's emotions – ranging from anger to delight (eg Gen 6:6).

"Top 10" Emotional Needs

We all have the same basic emotional needs:

Attention	Comfort	Acceptance	Approval	Appreciation
Encouragement	Support	Security	Affection	Respect

Think about two of these 'Top 10'. In what specific ways could you meet the emotional needs of your family members, colleagues or neighbours? – 1 Thess 5:11

"The Emotional Cup"

We may have emotions such as hurt, guilt, anxiety, stress, anger, depression or fear. It is a myth that, if you love someone, you will never feel angry with them.

Emptying the cup through confession and forgiveness. Forgiveness is the only way to be free from hurt and resentment. Is there anybody you need to forgive from your heart? – Eph 4:31

Day Four

Healing emotions can be difficult

There are ways of healing emotions through meeting relational needs, but there are reasons why we can find this difficult.

Comforting Those Who Mourn
Weeping with those who weep.

Listening
Caring supportive relationships – removing aloneness

Who of your relatives, colleagues or neighbours could you listen to in an accepting, non-judgemental way?

Taking Responsibility for our Choices
Nobody can *make* you angry – your emotions, attitudes and reactions are your own.

Unforgiveness in a relationship hardens the heart.

Communication 'roadblocks' include criticising, nagging, shouting, complaining, threatening, and sarcasm.

Day Five

Practical methods to build healthy relations

There are practical ways of managing our emotions to build positive, healthy relationships in our families, in the church, in the communities in which we live, and at work. We can develop an action plan which will give us a way forward.

Resolving conflict
Listen to the other person's point of view and feelings first, ensuring they feel heard and understood before you state yours. Feelings are more powerful than issues – deal with them first. – Rom 12:10

Is there anybody with whom you have an outstanding disagreement? What are you going to do about it?

"Building Relationships"
Good relationships are built on care and trust, with vulnerable communication, joint accomplishment and mutual giving.

Some of the material for these seminars is taken from D&T Ferguson, Intimate Life Ministries.

Books

Make Anger Your Ally, Neil Clark Warren (Tyndale)
The Great Commandment Principle, David Ferguson (Tyndale)*
Top 10 Intimacy Needs, Dr David Ferguson and Dr Don McMinn (Intimacy Press)*
The Truths We Must Believe, Dr Chris Thurman (Thomas Nelson)

* *Available from Intimate Life Ministries, St Mark's Church, Rugby Rd, Leamington Spa, CV32 6DL*

DON'T RETIRE – GET RETREADED

Day Two

"Things Ain't What They Used to Be"

1. Perspectives on Age
Biblical.
Chronological.
Social.
Functional.
Commercial.
Athletic – too old at 20!
Personal – how old are you really? How old do you feel – act – live?

2. Age Concerns
Declining strength. As we start slowing down, we may get anxious about our future.
Financial constraints. How do we cope as prices rise and our incomes stay the same?
Loneliness. Bereavement and health concerns can reduce our ability to participate, and the circle of friends can grow smaller. What can we do?

3. Attitudes to Older People
In society. Does Western society devalue the worth of the elderly?
In the media. How are older people portrayed?
In the family. We may feel that we are a burden.
In the church. Tragically, in many churches the attitude is little different from that of society.

4. Temptations of Age
Resistance to change.
Rocking chair mentality – feeling that it's time for someone else to do their bit.
Nothing more to learn.
Superglue leaders – staying in control when we should have stepped down years ago.
Romancing the past. Were they really so good, those days gone by?
Regrets, guilt, bitterness. Live in God's forgiveness here and now.
Self-pity. May be due to vulnerability or feeling redundant.
God seems far away. Keep active in the spiritual disciplines.

Day Three

"Stay Young and Beautiful"

Physical
Health. What is the Bible's perspective on taking care of our bodies?
Fitness. Does it matter what shape we are in?
Leisure.
Diet. Am I really what I eat?

Mental
Educational opportunities.

Sexual
You may have snow on the roof, but it doesn't mean the fire's gone out in the boiler!

Recreational
There is such a lot that can be done for the community and much that is offered to older people by the community. Take the opportunity to learn something new and do something different.

Spiritual
Keep fit spiritually, stay alive in God, seek a place of service, keep on learning.

Books
Just Fiona (video), Fiona Castle (CTA / Care for the Family)
Grandparenting, ed Joan King (NCEC)
Free to Grieve, Maureen Rank (Bethany House)
As our Years Increase, Tim Stafford (IVP)
Ageing, General Synod report produced by Anglican Board of Social Responsibility (Church House Publishing)
The Last Lap, John Eddison (Kingsway)
Dying to Live, Jim Graham (Marshall Pickering)
A Death in the Family, Jean Richardson (Lion)

Day Four

"Somewhere Over the Rainbow"

Our Perspective

What is the Biblical perspective on death and eternity?

Final arrangements

What preparation has been made in advance for the funeral, thanksgiving service? Cremation or burial? Do your relatives and friends know your wishes about hymns, speaker?

Grieving

The various stages of grieving: shock, anger, guilt, regret, fantasy, blame, reality.

Support for the bereaved:

Listen to them	Encouragement
Commitment that is long term	Talking
Contact – touch	Prayer is important
Encouragement in rebuilding life	Friendship
Crying and laughing together	Practical support

Memories – help to release memories and learn to talk things through

Our Personal Preparation

Are we ready to meet Jesus? The return of Jesus – will he really come back to earth? Is heaven a reality to us?

Day Five

"Onward, Christian Soldiers"

Keep on Growing

Growth requires challenge and challenge leads to change. Don't give up the basics – Bible reading, prayer, Christian fellowship – and recognise the importance of pastoral support and seek it.

Keep on Serving

Biblical and historical examples.
In the church – Explore with your church leaders what place of service you can have in the life of your church.
In society – What skills and abilities do you possess that will be of value in the local community?
In mission – Can you offer your services for short term missionary activity?
In your home.

Keep on Sharing

We are all called to be witnesses. You have a story to tell; are you sharing it?

Keep on Learning

Have you ever read the Bible through from Genesis to Revelation? Take a personal walk through the Bible.

Keep on Fighting

We cannot afford to coast. We are involved in a spiritual conflict with a diabolically intelligent enemy. Keep your helmet pulled down and your shield up - you really are part of the true 'Dad's Army.'

Keep on Running

Perseverance – Christian life involves us in a marathon; we reach the final tape through committed persistence with our eyes fixed on the Lord Jesus. Don't quit or get sidetracked.

FAMILY IN CHURCH & SOCIETY

What do 'family values' mean when the divorce rate nears 50%? When increasing numbers of children are born out of wedlock? When gay partnerships are placed on a par with marriage? And how does this relate to Biblical standards? These sessions will explore God's purpose for families.

Day Two

Family and Culture: Then and Now

In this session we examine the social factors which shape family life.

The prevailing cultural worldview
A culture which believes in faithfulness, commitment and mutual self-giving will produce a different model of family from one which is committed to individualism, self-serving and the centrality of money.

Media representations
Ranging from Waltons-style nostalgia to the grim adultery, abuse and incest featured in several current soaps.

Ethnic and class distinctions vs. universal traits
We have to find a healthy balance between culture-specific and global family values.

Attitudes to marriage
As Christians we often find ourselves promoting marriage while dealing on the ground with the consequences of marital breakdown. This can create tensions.

The family in the West today
The social upheaval of the 1960s led many to question the validity of the family.

The singles explosion
The phenomenal growth in the proportion of those living alone.

Day Three

Family in Scripture and Theology

In the Old Testament
History begins with a family (Gen 1:28), and redemption is promised through Abraham's descendants (Gen 12:3, 17:3–14). 'Family' in the Old Testament means more than blood-ties. Foreigners are incorporated into the 'family' of Israel (Deut 21:10), and the alien, the fatherless and the widow are to benefit from the family's estate.

In the New Testament
Jesus was born into a family and lived a family life. He gladly embraced the hospitality of families and enjoyed the company of children (Mark 1:31; Matt 19:14). By calling God 'Abba' (dear Father), he modelled devotional life on the pattern of family relationships.

Too often, however, we have equated the biblical picture with narrowly defined norms (e.g. the nuclear family). This can be detrimental to mission in a society now characterised by a wider variety of models (single, single parent, adoptive, extended, live-in grandparents etc.).

In Christian doctrine
The trinity is the true 'First Family'. Father and Son cooperate to effect reconciliation with a broken world. Believers are incorporated into his family by adoption (Eph 1:5; Rom.8:23). The criterion of membership is now faith rather than ancestry (Jn 1:12–13), but physical families are still crucial for the proper functioning of Christian communities (Acts 16:33–4; Rom 16:3ff.).

It is right to look, if we are serious about strengthening the family life, at how we can support the institution of marriage.
– Tony Blair

It is misleading and unhelpful to talk of the 'Christian family'. In reality, there is no such thing. It is more accurate to say that there are families, some of which are Christian. The challenges and difficulties faced in the home by Christians are exactly the same as those with which other people struggle.
– John and Olive Drane

Day Four

Family and Politics

The family never exists in isolation. It relates to the rest of society and as such is reflected in the law, in economic and social policies and in political programmes.

Current party policies on the family

Global policies on the family

The influence and work of the United Nations. The impact of international trade patterns, health provision and educational funding.

Christian policies on the family

The strategy and work of Christian organisations.

The legacy of the 1960s

Their continuing effect on current political and ethical debate about the family.

Feminism and the family

The children's rights movement

Scripture often emphasises the protection of children, but the question of their 'rights' is more open to debate.

Education and the family

How far can state schools be expected to uphold Christian family values, in a pluralist culture?

Day Five

Family and Church

Family and church in church history

The movement away from family to 'institutional' and 'state' churches. Community models. The feminist critique of 'patriarchal' church government.

Family and the 21st century church

The challenge of newer forms of church: cells, homogeneous units, youth churches.

The church and singleness

Is the 'church family'/'family church' an unhelpful concept for singles?

Family, church and the '24 hour society'

The pressure to re-organise church around expanded working days, the decreasingly 'special' nature of Sundays, and busier and more complex family schedules.

With Christ at the centre of our homes, we can make a difference. We can be there for the casualties. We can make our presence felt in society, showing by the way we live that there is a better way.

– Robert Ireton

Books

I Believe in the Family, Gary Collins, (Hodder and Stoughton)
Families at the Crossroads, Rodney Clapp (IVP)
Happy Families?, John and Olive Drane (Harper Collins)
A Passion for the Family, Robert Ireton (Hodder and Stoughton)

Day Two

Building a Successful Marriage

The Foundation of a Successful Marriage: Covenant

The basis for a working marriage is 'wanting your good at my expense'. Covenant faithfulness is the bedrock of successful marriages.

The Cement of a Successful Marriage: Leaving and Cleaving

One flesh can only be achieved through leaving and cleaving. What, whom and how are we leaving? What, to whom and how are we cleaving? (Gen 2:18–25; Matt 19:4–8).

Unloading the baggage - dealing with the issues of parents and their control, past relationships, divorce, cohabitation.

The Walls of a Successful Marriage: Developing Trust

Trust is not a gift, it is earned. How can we develop trust in our relationships? (Ps 37:3; Ps 52:8).

The Atmosphere of a Successful Marriage: Forgiveness

The oil of forgiveness builds healthy relationships, releasing joy and fun, as opposed to strain and stress. (2 Cor 2:10–11; Eph 4:15–31; Matt 18:21–35).

The Attitude of a Successful Marriage: Servanthood

Developing a selfless lifestyle in the midst of a self-centred society.

Husbands are to love their wives as Christ loved the Church. How can we achieve this? (Eph 5:22–33).

Wives are to bring credit to God's word by their lifestyle. Is this possible? (Titus 2:5–8)

Day Three

The Language of Love

What's She on About? Understanding Each Other's Love Languages

It can be a struggle to get on each other's wave-length. We can appreciate our differences and recognise we are NOT the same.

There are different ways of expressing love…but which is the right one? Speech… touch… hearing… romance… practical work… etc.

Bedroom or Boredroom? Sexual Love

What is different for Christians? Understanding how we are made. Is anything off-limits for the Christian?

Setting the right tone, creating a comfortable environment.

Motives: giving not getting.

Unhurried time together. Rediscovering fun and pleasure. Creativity – surprise and humour help to retain freshness.

Kiss and Make Up? Conflict – The Loving Way

Correction not rejection. Understand we can be corrected and yet still loved.

Listening – or hearing? Are we really getting the message our partner is trying to convey? Are the issues we discuss producing change, or do we just rehearse the same old problems?

The art of compromise. Learning the 'win-win' syndrome. The grace of yielding to each other for harmony's sake. The place of prayer in conflict.

Day Four

Troubled Waters

First Things First: Priorities

How do we prioritise our worlds? Partners – children – church – work.

It is written@ bible.god. Deut 10:12–13.

Money Matters: Finances

The acquisition and use of money. How and why do we make it? How and where do we use it?

Sharing our money. Do we discuss this rationally or argue it passionately?

It is written@ bible.god. Matt 5:19–24.

It's Been A Hard Day's Night: Work

The Company demands. Who owns our soul? What really is important and who decides?

Keeping our integrity in a shady environment.

Keeping an eye on the clock – how much time is right? Who gets my best time and why? The fear of failure and possible unemployment.

It is written@ bible.god. Eph 6:5–9; Col 3:22–4:1.

Families At War? Family

Handling the pressures of parenthood.

Coping with the intrusions of family, work mates and your teenagers' undesirable aquaintances. Step-families. Handling the difficulties that can arise.

Dependent older relatives. The responsibility that can add stress to your marriage.

It is written@ bible.god. Prov 2:1–4; 22:6; Matt 19:4–6; Mk 7:9–13.

In Sickness and in Health: Physical Well-being

The challenge of ill-health in the family. How can we prepare? How will we respond?

It is written@ bible.god. Prov 18:14; Jas 5:13–16.

Day Five

Marriage MOT

Everything You've Ever Wanted to Ask... But Daren't! Sixty Minutes Question Time

An opportunity to develop the issues raised and fill in the gaps from the week's ministry, with panel and audience participation.

Marriage M.O.T. Time: Personal Goal Setting for Our Marriages

What has God been revealing to you this week?

What positive steps can you begin to make?

What do you hope to add to your marriage by this time next year?

Books

Leaving the Light On, Gary Smalley and John Trent (Nelson Word)
Ten Principles For a Happy Marriage, Selwyn Hughes (Marshall Pickering)
How To Make Love To The Same Person For The Rest Of Your Life, Dagmar O'Connor (Bantam)
Tender Love, Bill Hybels and Rob Wilkins (Moody)
Getting Your Sex Life Off To a Great Start, Penner and Penner (Word)
Intended For Pleasure, Ed Wheat and Gaye Wheat (Scripture Union)
Marriage Takes More Than Love, Jack and Carole Marshall (Navpress)
The Sixty Minute Marriage, Rob Parsons (Hodder and Stoughton)

Family life is a mixture of fun and frustration, pleasure and pain, good times and bad times. Parenting is the most valuable and important job we'll ever do. There is no blueprint for perfect parenting – we're unique as parents and in what we can offer to our children. Remember, it's never too late to make changes.

Day Two

Positive Investment in our Children

Learning how to base our parenting on a foundation of unconditional love – 'love without strings' – and communicating that love to our children.

Love without strings means not forcing our expectations on them, but encouraging their individual gifts and ambitions.

Develop their emotional security by building an emotional bank account.

Do we build them up (noticing their effort and improvement; encouraging them; having a positive attitude), or put them down (criticising, nagging, embarrassing them, comparing them to others).

Time management – with the family as a whole and with the various individuals.

Actions are important – demonstrations of love, physical touch, looks, attitudes, etc.

Day Three

Don't Just Stand There... Say Something!

Children have a right to ask that we earn their respect. We do not have the right automatically, but the benefits of mutual respect, love and honesty in communication are beyond price.

Listening skills – picking up the signals. To listen well, we can: – stop what we are doing – listen attentively – make an effort to understand – be slow to talk – reflect back to them what we think they are saying

Say what you mean and mean what you say.

How to recognise and handle feelings – coping with anger, handling and not denying emotions.

Communication of values, family history and beliefs, and sharing our own experiences.

"We never know the love of a parent until we become parents ourselves."
– Henry Ward Beecher

EMOTIONAL BANK ACCOUNT

year	credit	£	debit	£
1	Attend to needs Hugs and kisses Singing	100 100 50	Not enough attention	100
2	Walk in the park Say "I love you"	50 100	Get told off	50
3	Reading a book together Romp in the garden	50 50	Can't do what they want	50
4	Comfort when upset	100	Jealous of new baby	100
5	Play football	50	School worries	100
6	Be interested in school Take time to really talk	100 100	Get no encouragement Move house/school	100 100
7	Help with homework	100	Mum blows her cool	50
8	Play a game	50	Bullied at school	100
9	Go on a bike ride	50		
10	Talk about growing up	50	Compared with brother/sister	100
11	Go to a football match	50	Get poor school marks	100
12	Encouragement Give info on sexuality	100 100	Have row Not listened to	50 100
13	Listen to more problems	100	Parents argue	100
14	Accept for who they are	100		
15	Talk over relationship problem Share your life experience	100 100	Can't talk about worries Row with boy/girl friend	100 100
16	Test for exams	100	Parents are unfair	50
17	Discuss their future	100	Feel depressed	100
18	Let them go	200		

Day Four

Setting Loving Limits

There is no parenthood or fulfilled childhood without discipline. "It hurts me more than it hurts you", we say to our children, but without loving discipline, both child and parent will hurt much more.

What is discipline? Understanding a clear definition.

Why do children misbehave? It could be a result of inadequacy, peer pressure, attention seeking, a power contest, revenge, boredom, or a lack of boundaries. All of these can be addressed in different ways.

Why can it be so hard to discipline our children? We may be too tired, lack confidence, feel guilty, or not have the time.

Our children need the security of loving limits – setting boundaries.

Handling difficult behaviour. We can allow children to make choices and learn from the consequences of their behaviour.

Day Five

Roots and Wings

Every Christian parent worries that their children will reject the faith that they hold dear. Whilst every child has to make his or her own decision, the way we handle teaching our children can be a pivot or a put-off. If they have a loving, affectionate, listening parent, it will help them form an image of a loving God.

We are stewards of our children, not their owners.

Setting the example - being a positive role model. We may feel guilty that we can never measure up to our own ideals, but just the fact that we keep on loving God through our everyday lives will speak volumes.

Releasing them to make choices – giving them responsibility.

Being naturally spiritual – developing a sense of wonder, and building celebrations and rituals into our family life.

Family worship – developing a living prayer life – using God's word to guide, inspire and empower our children in their everyday lives.

"Almighty God and heavenly Father, we thank you for the children which you have given us: give us also grace to train them in your faith, fear and love; that as they advance in years they may grow in grace, and may hereafter be found in the number of your elect children."
– John Cosin

Books

The Special Years, Celia Bowring (Kingsway)
How to Really Love Your Child, Ross Campbell (Victor)
How to Build Confidence in Your Child, Dr James Dobson (Kingsway)
Power to Parent, Sue Smith (Hodder)
The Parentalk Guide to the Toddler Years, Steve Chalke (Hodder)
The Parentalk Guide to the Childhood Years, Steve Chalke (Hodder)
The Sixty Minute Mother, Rob Parsons (Hodder)
Raising Compassionate, Courageous Children in a Violent World, Dr Janice Cohn
Creating Kids who can Concentrate, Jean Robb, Hilary Letts
The Family Dinner Game, Family Caring Trust

PARENTING 11+s

Explore the world of being a parent and delve into the feeling of being a child, with the aim of enabling us all to be better parents.

On this subject, we are all expert failures! If you looking for success, you won't find it here – but what you will find is realism, empathy, trust and hopefully some answers.

Day Two

Love Them

Love Them and Let Them Know

Give love without strings – love them 'anyway'. We may not love what they do, but we love them because they are our child.

Children need security, self worth and significance. We provide security when we love our children unconditionally. We build self-worth when we respect them and their opinions. Giving them significance involves trusting them and giving increasing responsibility as they grow up.

Tell them you love them, and show them you love them.

Being A Master Builder – Beware of Demolition

Catch them doing something right. Try to encourage them and praise their effort, thoughtfulness, right intention and motive.

Build them up with time, touch and tenderness. Protect your time with them and let them know they are important.

Day Three

Know them

Know Their World

Unlocking the world of older children. What every kid wished their parents knew - and vice versa.

How well do you know your child? A revealing questionnaire!

Are you listening? How to listen badly and how to listen well. Remember it's good to talk. "Consider that God gave us two ears and only one mouth so that we listen twice as much as we talk."

"If only God would lean out of heaven and tell me [that my children] are going to make it, I could relax. But God doesn't do that. He tells us to be the parents he has called us to be in his strength and promises to do his part. Driven to prayer, ... I began to realize I was only truly positive and confident when I'd been flat on my face before the Lord."

– Jill Briscoe

Books

How to Really Love Your Teenager, Ross Campbell (Victor)
How to Succeed as a Parent, Steve Chalke (Hodder)
The Parentalk Guide to the Teenage Years, Steve Chalke (Hodder)
Why Do They Do That?, Nick Pollard (Lion)
Teenagers – The Parent's One-Hour Survival Guide, Paul Francis (Harper Collins)
What Every Kid Wished Their Parents Knew... and Vice Versa!, Rob and Lloyd Parsons (Hodder)
The Sixty Minute Father, Rob Parsons (Hodder)
The Sixty Minute Parent (video), Rob Parsons (Care for the Family)

Day Four

Defend them

Defend the Boundaries

When boundaries are crossed... take action. Say what you mean and mean what you say.

When we set boundaries we need to know how, why and for whose benefit. Discipline is about providing security, self-worth and stability. Children need to feel unconditionally loved for discipline to be effective. Find a plan that fits the child and the problem... tailor made. Be realistic, reasonable, firm and flexible.

Choose your battles. Does this really matter? Know when to forgive, say sorry and move on.

When It All Goes Wrong...

Is it really the end of the world? Get the story straight – take a sharp intake of breath, keep calm and go for a long walk.

Keep loving them anyway.

Don't hide – share and surround yourself with good friends.

Day Five

Nurture them

Back to the Future

It's never too late to build memories to last a lifetime.

Remember the power of laughter.

Build family routines and traditions – they give a strong basis of love and a sense of belonging.

Sharing Your Faith - Praying for Your Children

Copycat – how like us are they. What are they catching from us?

Involving others.

When families pray.

Parenting with Elastic! You Must Let Them Go

"Worrying is like a rocking chair; it gives you something to do, but it doesn't get you anywhere."

Let go from the very beginning – find ways to 'stretch the elastic'.

Don't delegate the big issues – if you don't tell them, someone else will.

Give them the freedom to make mistakes.

A word on the empty nest.

Parenting MOT

How often do you have a check up? Make some decisions and create some surprises!

"There is just one way to bring up a child in the way he should go and that is to travel that way yourself."
– *Abraham Lincoln*

Day Two

Singleness – God's will?

The will of God

Is it God's will that I remain single? (cf Jesus on 'eunuchs' and Paul on 'advantages of singleness'). He sees the pain of involuntary singleness.

And yet we are all called to be single – at least for a while. So let's work out how we can be happily single today. 'I have learned the secret of being content in any and every situation.' – Phil 4:12

Is there one person that God intends me to marry?

What methods did our Jewish and Christian predecessors use to help their young find marriage partners?

How do other modern cultures deal with the complexities of finding a marriage partner? Sometimes what we think of as our theology is just our culture. Decision making and the will of God.

How is this affecting the Kingdom of God?

Involuntary singleness can lead to:

The distraction of the perpetual search for a partner.
Low morale.
Immorality.
Marrying someone because there's no-one else.

Beware the lies and believe the truth:

Marriage is not a guaranteed cure for loneliness.
You can be happy without having sex.
Being single is not second-rate.

Day Three

Emotional Health

The state of our emotional health affects our ability to enjoy being single and make a good choice in marriage. Sometimes we say we want to find romance, but we run after unsuitable or unavailable people. Perhaps we are scared of being hurt again, or we do not have enough confidence that someone could possibly love us.

How emotional 'baggage' makes us unable to enjoy being single.

The distinction between raising self-esteem and pride. The mirage of seeking someone who will meet all our emotional needs.

How a weak self image creates havoc in our relationships with the opposite sex. We can't love anyone until we love ourselves.

How we can strengthen our 'inner person'

Decide not to wallow in passive self-pity.

Talk to church leaders and Christian friends about what you should do. If there's no expert advice in your church, don't be afraid to seek help elsewhere.

Seek God until you know how much he loves you.

Day Four

Sexuality and Singleness

We need to reclaim a right view of sex

Sex is an expression of commitment, rather than a route to it. It is also an instrument for creation.

Too much of the emphasis today is on using people as a commodity, with the focus on technique, not relationship.

In non-married relationships

How far is wise?

What is the best way to avoid going further than we want to? Don't be influenced by past mistakes or regrets.

We need to maintain respect for ourselves and our partners.

Masturbation

What does the Bible say?

Lust can become a habit – good sex is centred on someone else, not ourselves. But don't become paralysed by shame and isolation.

Homosexuality

The Bible, the church, and gay people.

What are the contributing causes?

Is celibacy the only option for Christian homosexuals?

Day Five

Finding Miss or Mr Right

Where are the best places to meet eligible Christians?

In our church, at other churches, Christian holidays, conferences etc.

Dating agencies – the theory and the practice! Making things happen ourselves.

How to say hello… the most difficult step in meeting people.

The pros and cons of dating a non-Christian.

What can you do to create community for single Christians… instead of waiting for your church leader to do something.

Books

The Single Issue, Al Hsu (IVP)
Beyond Singleness, Helena Wilkinson (IVP)
Single – the Jesus Model, Heather Wraight (IVP)
No Sex Please – We're Single!, Ian Stuart Gregory (Kingsway)
Suddenly Single, Phil Stanton (Kingsway)

CHILDREN WITH SPECIAL NEEDS

Parenting Children with Special Needs

There is such a range of special needs, from low-level to profound handicaps. The seminar will seek to focus on general issues, encouraging us all as parents to support and teach each other.

Family and Friends

How do your family, friends and church react? Are they supportive?

What are the difficulties… are they getting better?

Is it more difficult for Dads to work things through? Do they get emotional support? What helps them?

Day-to-Day Living

What helps you face the realities of the day?

One parent said, "Things are certainly difficult and not what we planned, but there are joys and triumphs to be had."

Can you relate to that statement at all? Or is your experience quite different?

What's the most difficult time of the day for you?

How can problems like this be overcome? What works?

The Positive Approach

"A special needs child achieves so much more than an ordinary child because they face so much challenge."

All children need to feel good about themselves and to feel loved by others. It's an issue that special needs children may really struggle with.

Does it matter if we often talk about the child's disability in front of him or her?

What does this feel like from their point of view?

How do we know when children don't feel good about themselves? Kids act out their feelings.

What can we do to help them feel more positive about themselves?

The Future

Do we include brothers and sisters when the future is talked about?

What does it feel like from their point of view?

Have we ever asked them if they feel guilty about being healthy themselves, or what their feelings are about the future?

Books

Extraordinary Kids, Cheri Fuller and Louise Tucker Jones (Focus on the Family)

PARENTS IN PAIN

"There is no pain like parental pain."

I've lost confidence in my ability to parent.

It's too late to go back and put it right.

I'm overwhelmed by the responsibility of it all.

This is a seminar to affirm, help, and above all, give hope.

The Guilt Trap

So often the word that best sums us up as parents is 'guilty.' It's so easy to feel that we have completely blown it.

This can immobilise us because we begin to lose confidence in our parenting. We are constantly saying to ourselves things like, "I dealt with that badly" or "I've blown it again." The truth is we do deal with things badly sometimes, but we're learning on the job as well.

The Pressure of Isolation

It's easy to feel that the difficulties we are going through are just us. Two of the most helpful words we can hear when we are doubting our ability as parents are, "me too."

Almost every parent – especially those whose children are in their late teens – wishes they could rewind the tape and have another run at it. The truth is we'd probably just make different mistakes.

Some issues we shall cover:

Is it our fault when children go off the rails?

How can we deal with children who seem to have rejected all we believe in?

Is there anything we can do to get ready for traumatic times that may be ahead with our children?

What do we do when we're in the middle of the crisis and there seems no way out?

Prodigal Sons and Daughters

Don't read the score at half time. There are some surprises in store for us with our kids.

Try to understand what it is they walked away from. Many 'prodigals' have not rejected God, but rather what they see as rules and regulations that have nothing to do with following Christ.

Re-establish the local church as a place of love and acceptance. "When the Father's house is filled with the Father's love, the prodigals will come home."

Love those that they love. The painful process of accepting and trying to love those people that matter to your child, even if they are not your idea of a good friend/partner/husband/wife.

Make sure you'll recognise it when they do come home. Sometimes our measure of spirituality is different to the one God uses.

Don't ever give up.

Books

Parents in Pain, Dr John White (IVP) – out of print
Why Do They Do That?, Nick Pollard (Lion)
Raising the Strong-Willed Child, Dr James Dobson (Kingsway)
What's So Amazing About Grace?, Philip Yancey (Zondervan)

SINGLE PARENTING

The Single Parent Journey

From 'broken-hearted to oaks of righteousness' – Is 61:1–3. Single parenting affects us emotionally, physically and spiritually. It is a journey which lasts a lifetime. We cannot go back to where we were before becoming a single parent. We are either stuck on this journey, or we can seek to move forward. Becoming a single parent usually involves crisis, shock and pain. There may also be relief from conflict, violence and abuse.

Loss

"Everything seemed to be taken away from me – my husband, my home, the family breadwinner, my security, my expectations, control over my own life." What are our losses?

Anger

Is it a sin? (Ps 4:4) It is a very powerful emotion. In anger we can harm others and ourselves. How do we deal with it positively and safely?

Rejection

One word covers so much pain. Jesus suffered the ultimate rejection on the cross (Matt 27:46). How can we accept love and learn to trust again?

Guilt

Have we sinned or have we been sinned against? Where is this guilt coming from?

Despair

Single parenting can be exhausting – a financial tightrope, a physical endurance test and an emotional rollercoaster. What does the future hold?

Climbing up

Who am I? Parent, nurse, teacher, housekeeper, gardener, handyman, decorator, taxi-service… God says: "You are precious and honoured in my sight… I love you." – Is 43:4

How can I Forgive?

Often those who have hurt us are not sorry. "Forgiveness may need to be a process. You may have to keep forgiving until the pain goes. How long is that? Until the pain goes." – *Rejection*, Steve Hepdon

How can I face Loneliness?

God sets the lonely in families (Ps 68:6).

24 Hour Parenting

All the pressures and issues of parenting, plus: Responsibility for all the day-to-day needs. No one to take over when you have flu, and one of the children has been sick all night. Making decisions, large and small. Finance. Paid employment vs full-time parent. Children's pain and confusion – they have emotions too. Not all the effects are negative.

Distance Parenting

Letting go, but building a different relationship. Consistent, caring contact.

Where is God and his Church?

Are single parents second class? Is there a place for single parent families in the church? How can we build better bridges within the Christian family? "Pure and genuine religion is this: to take care of orphans and widows in their suffering." – Jas 1:27

Books

Journey Through Single Parenting, Jill Worth with Christine Tufnell (Hodder and Stoughton)
Rejection, Steve Hepdon (Sovereign)
Parenting on Your Own, Lynda Hunter (Harper Collins)
Single Moments, Lynda Hunter (Tyndale)
From One Single Parent to Another, Sandra Aldrich (Regal)

NOTES

NOTES

NOTES